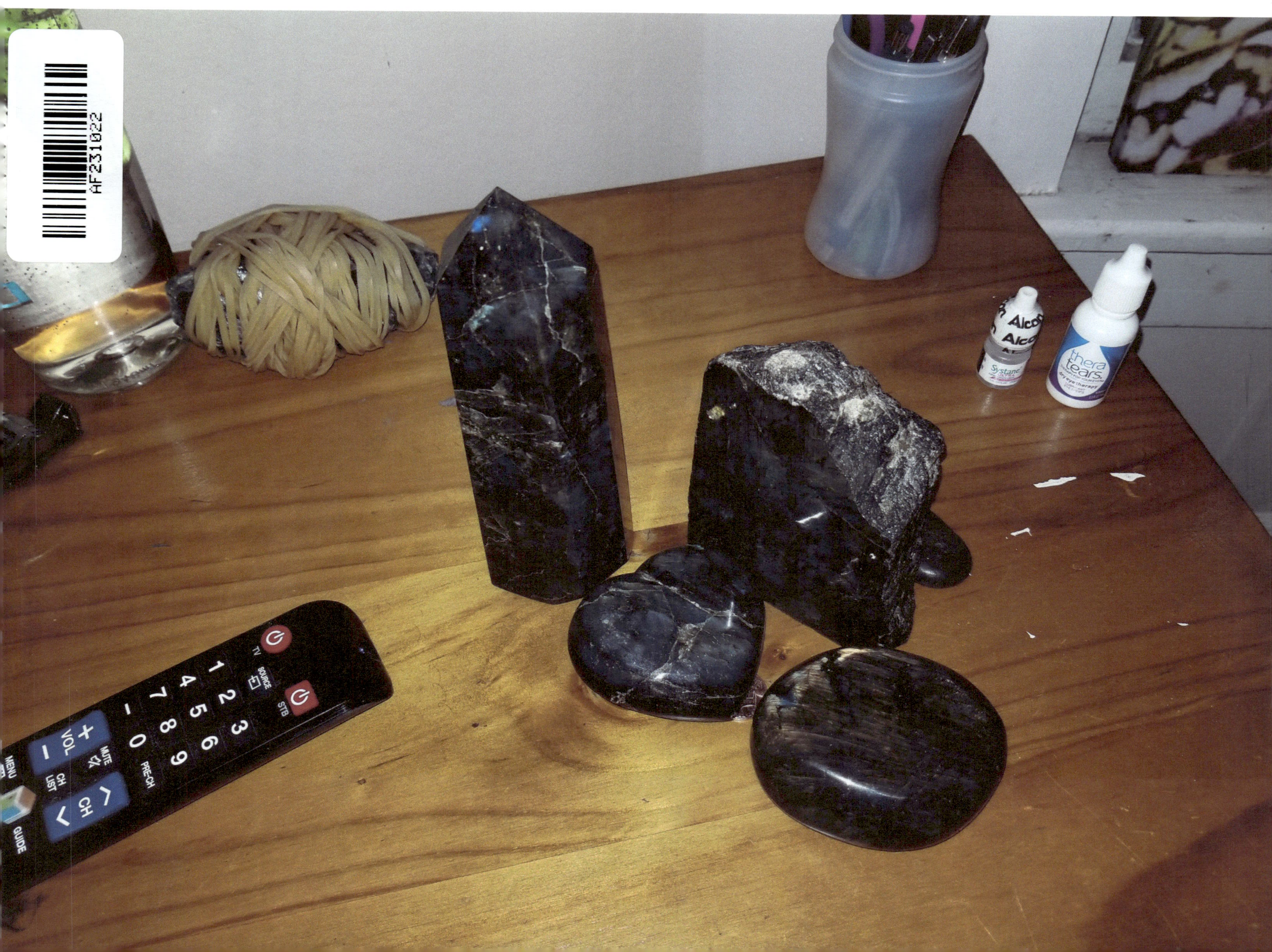
AF231022

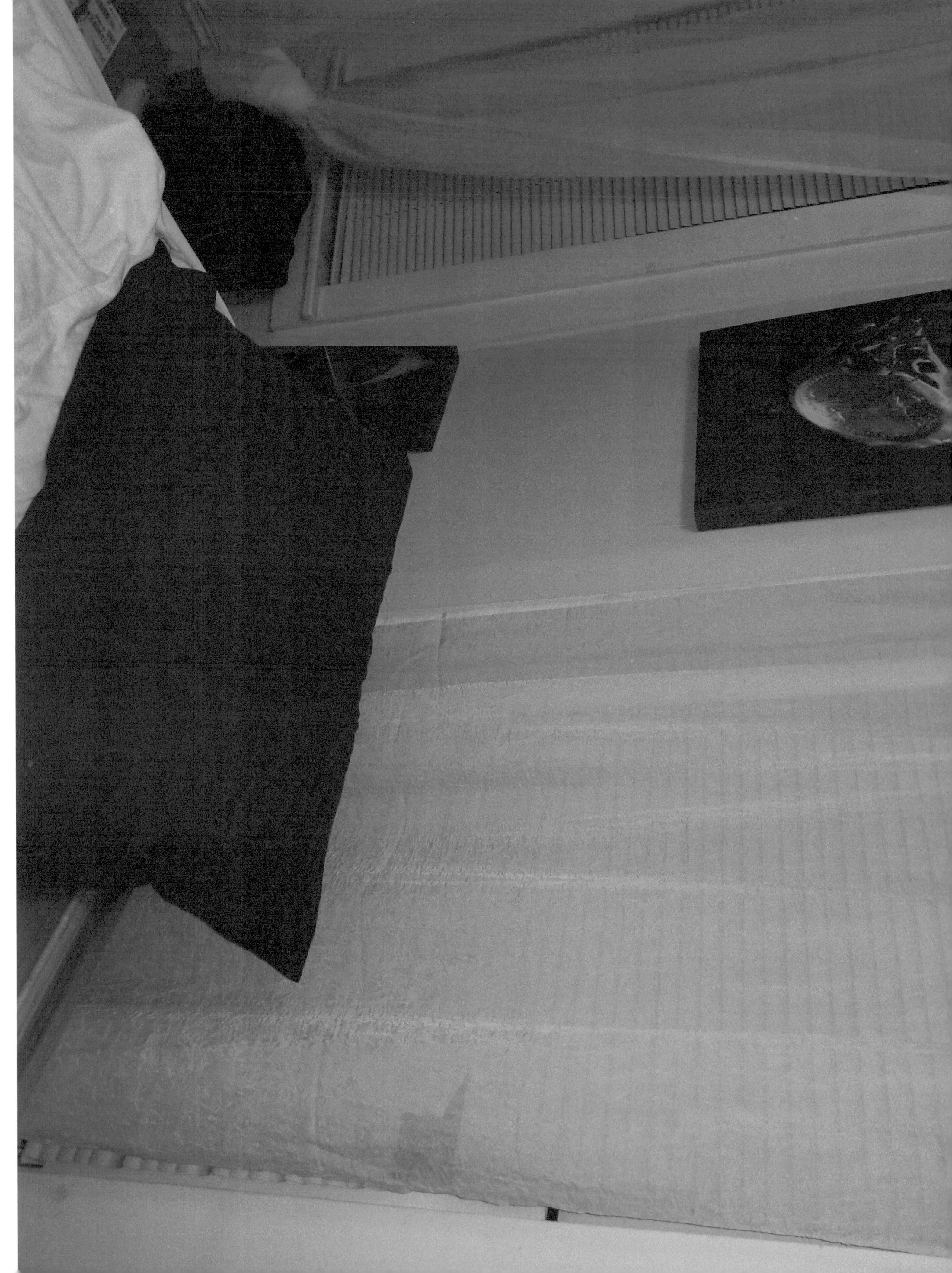

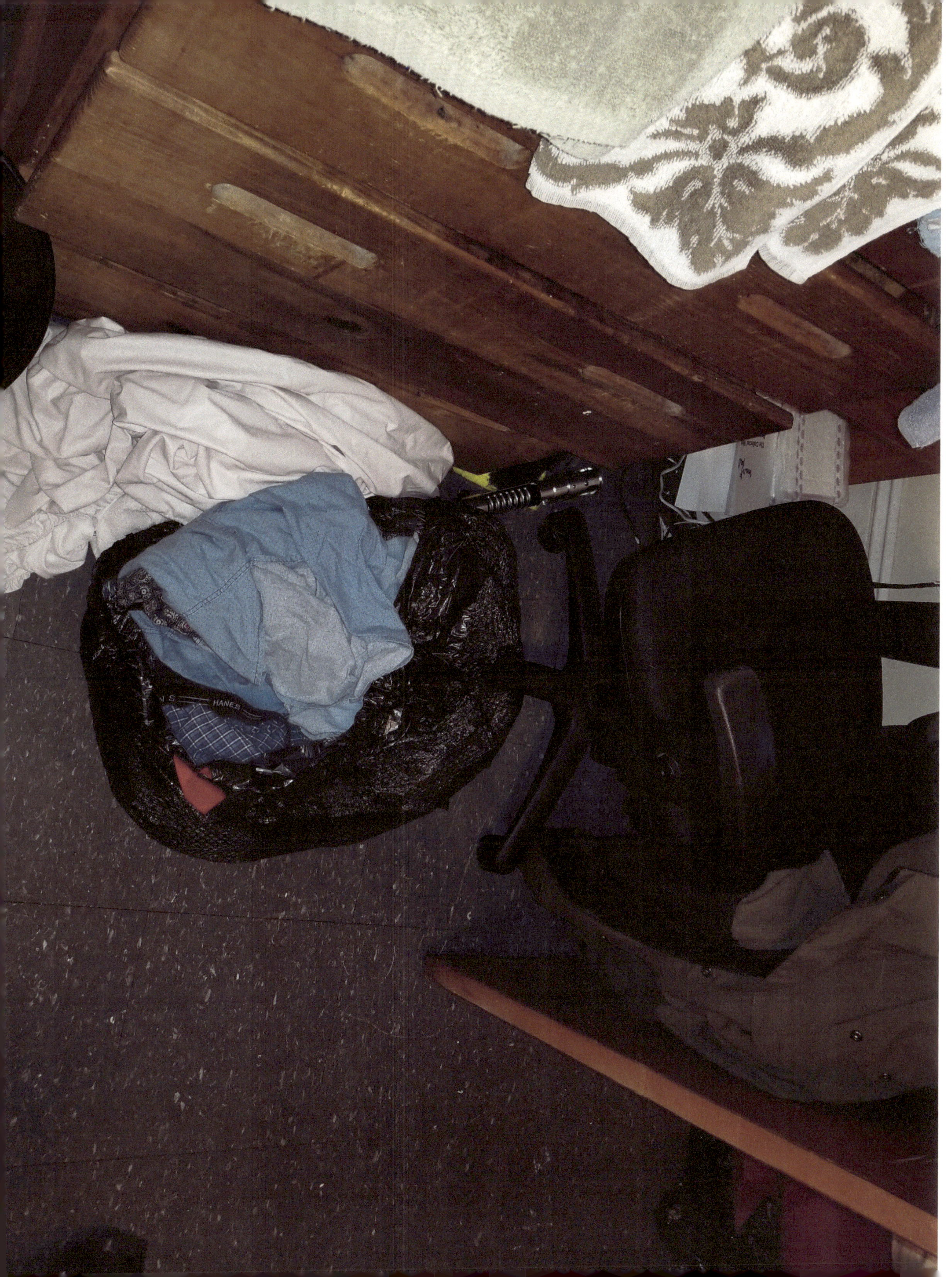

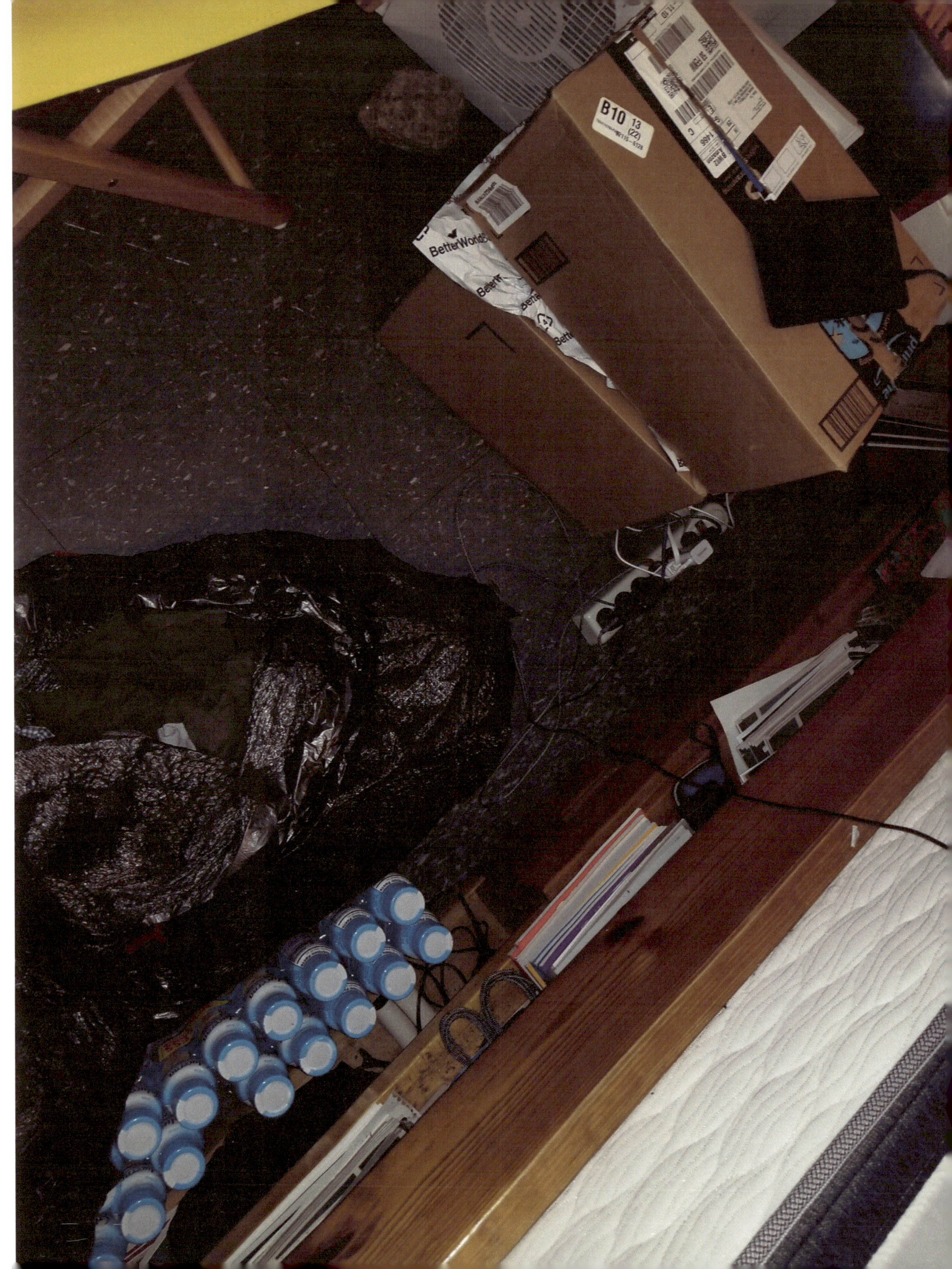

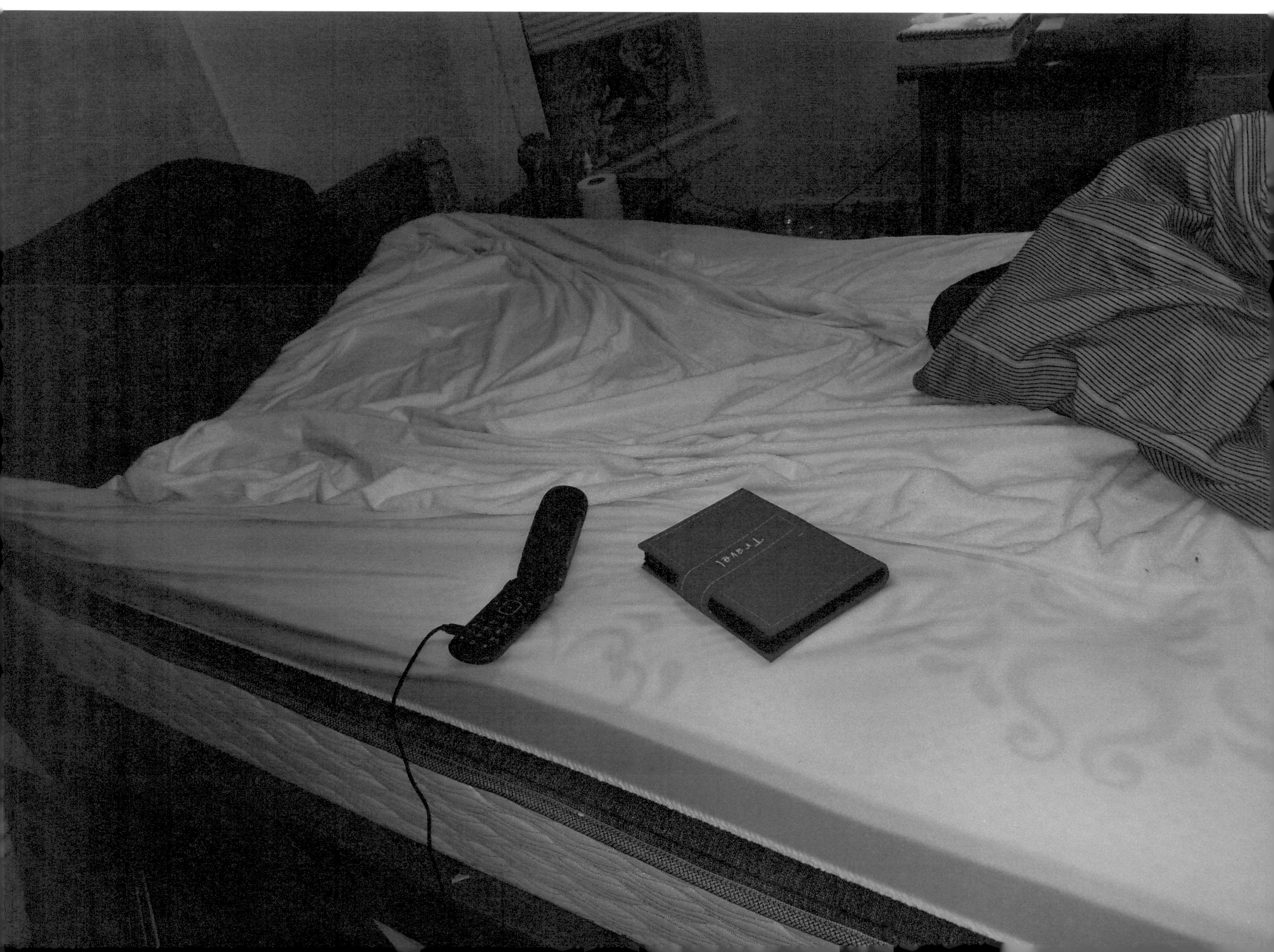
Travel

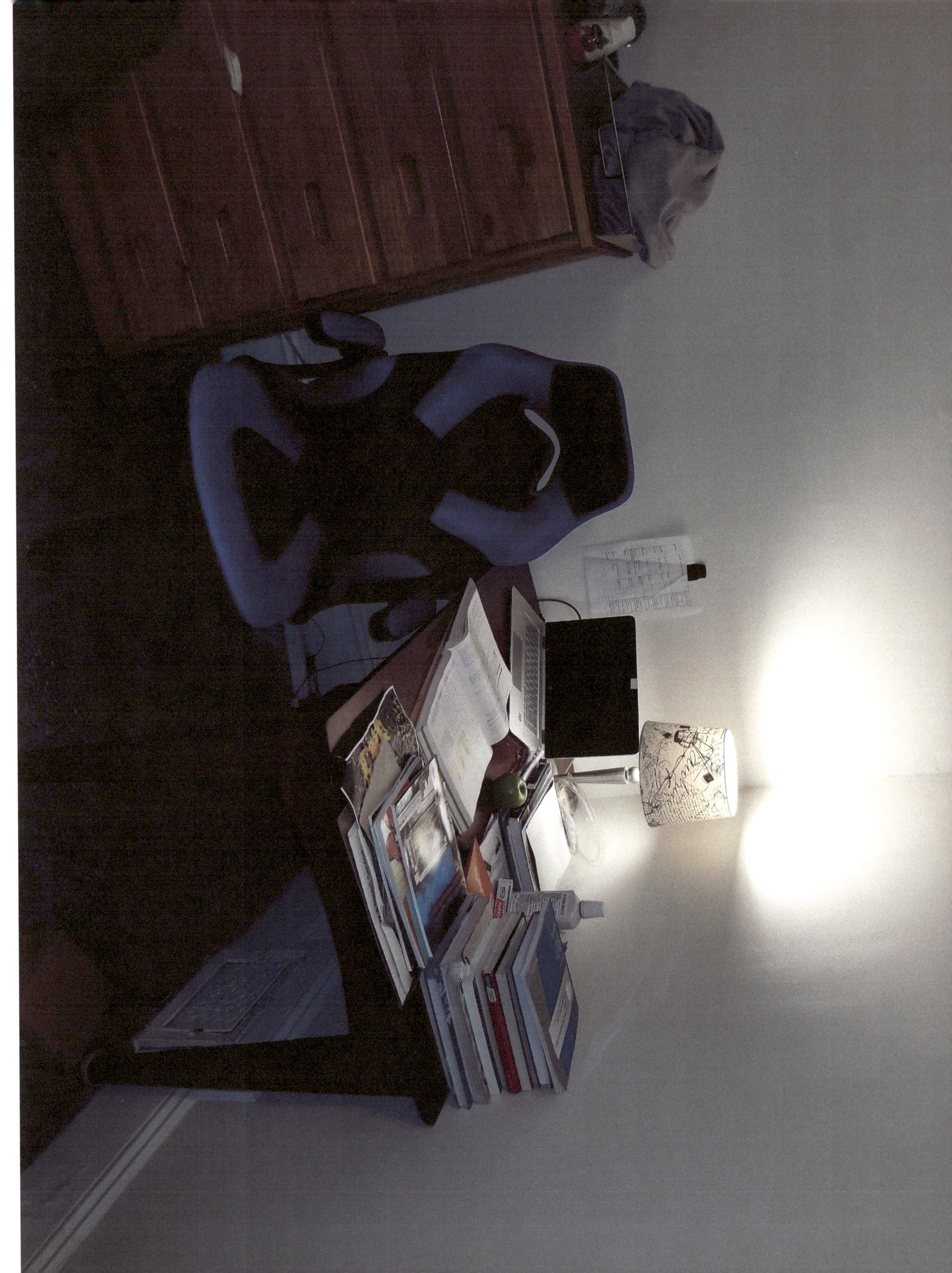

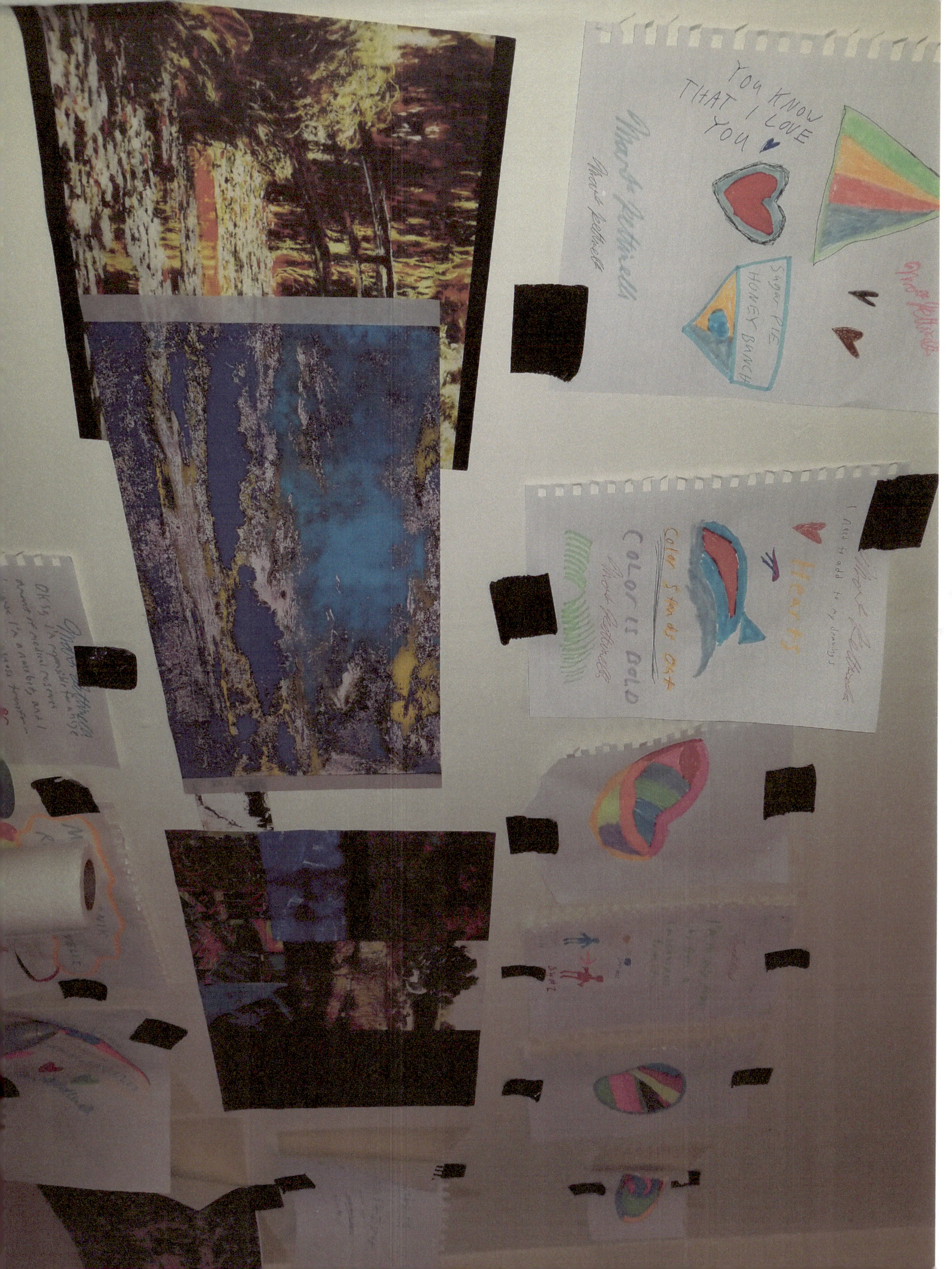
YOU KNOW
THAT I LOVE
YOU
Sugar PIE
HONEY BUNCH
COLOR is BOLD
Color Stands Out
Hearts

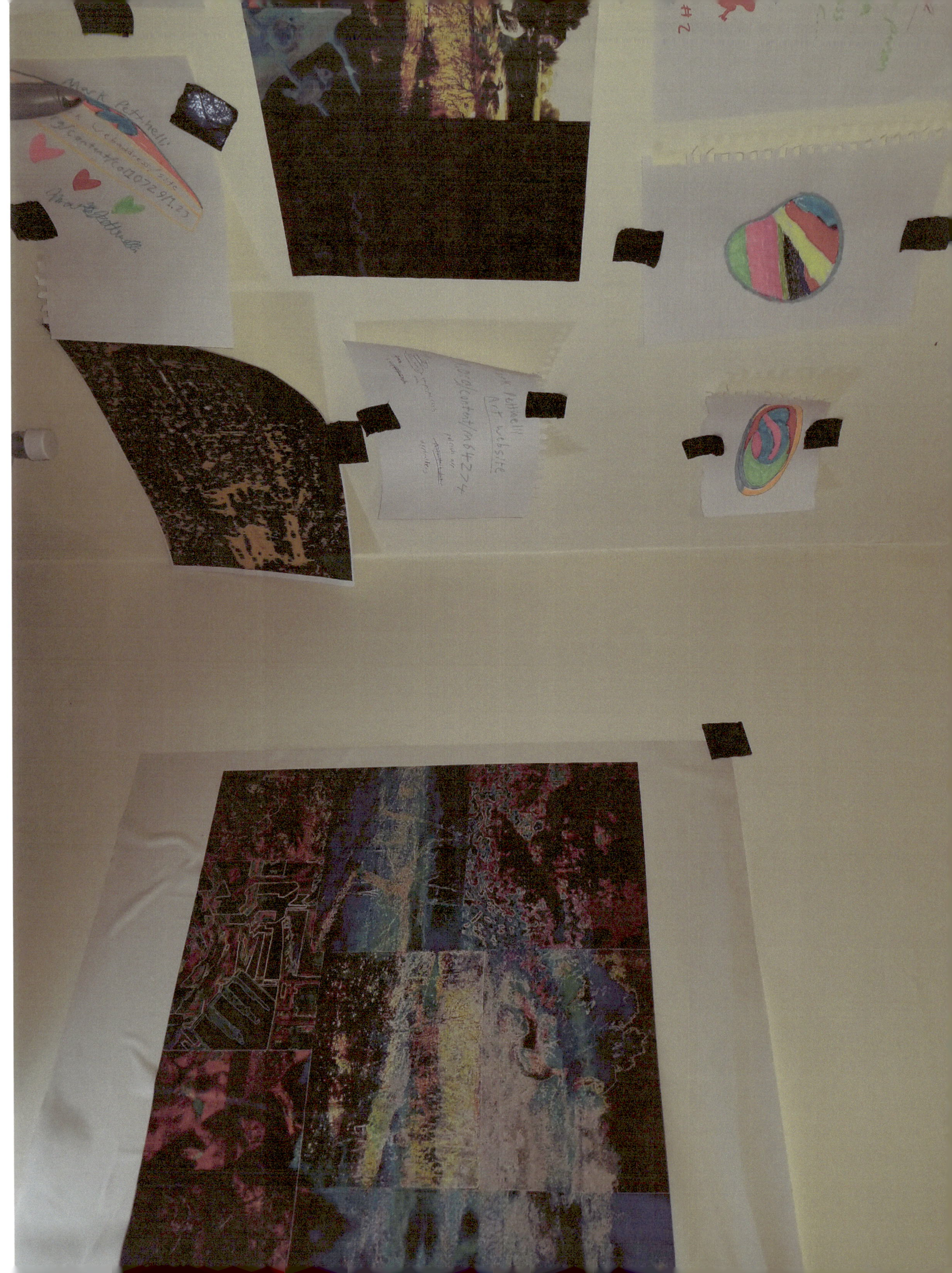

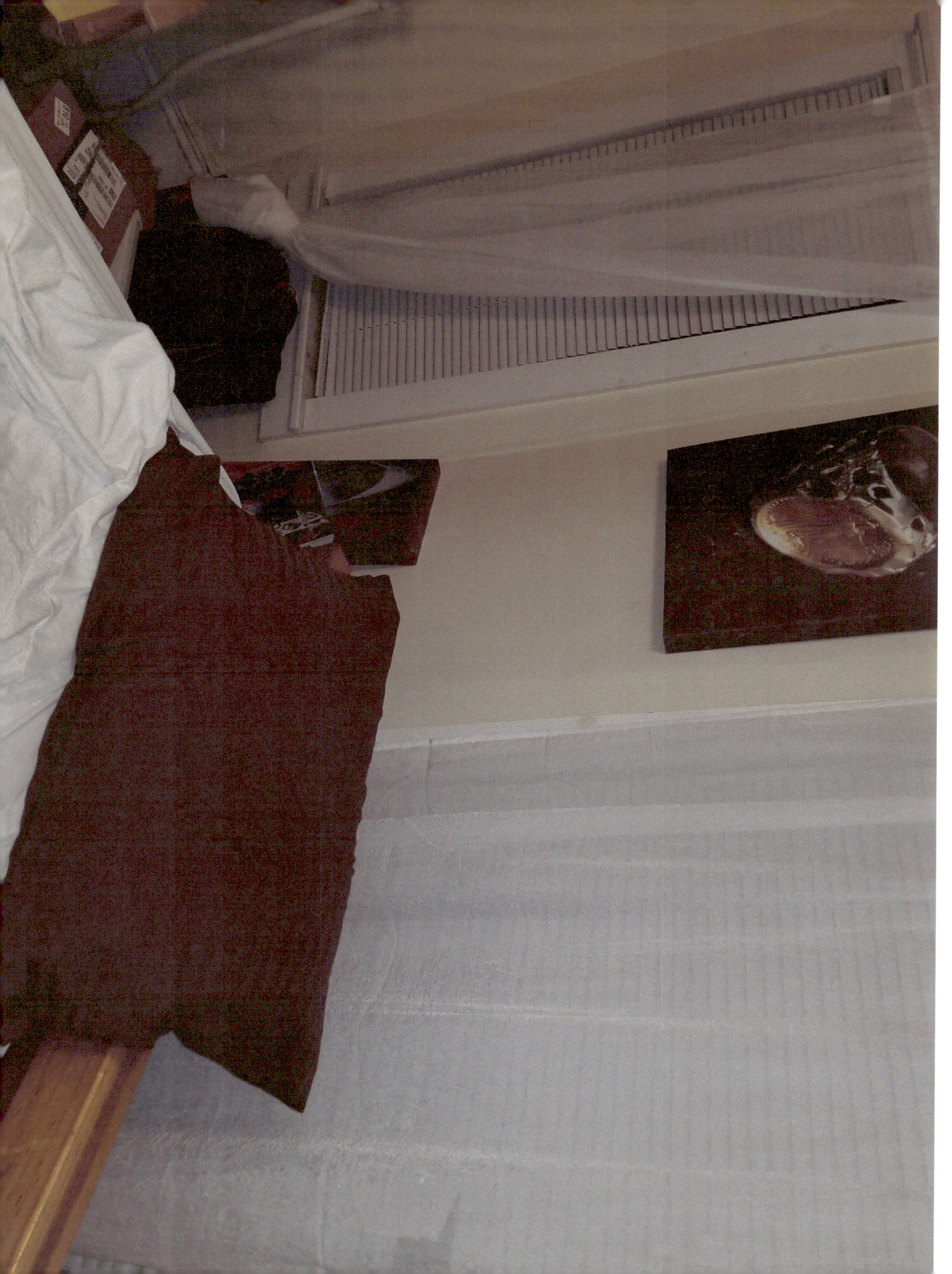

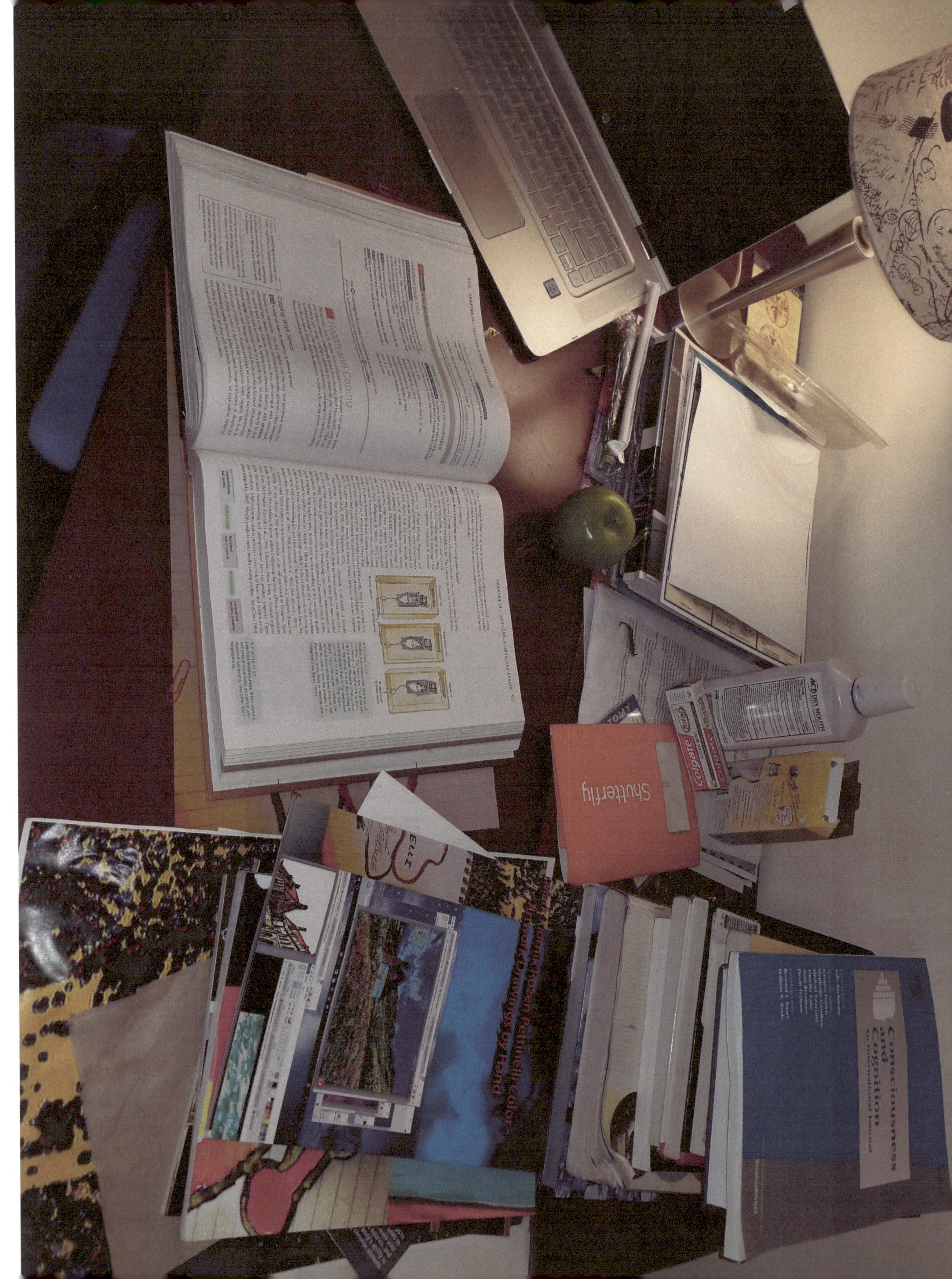

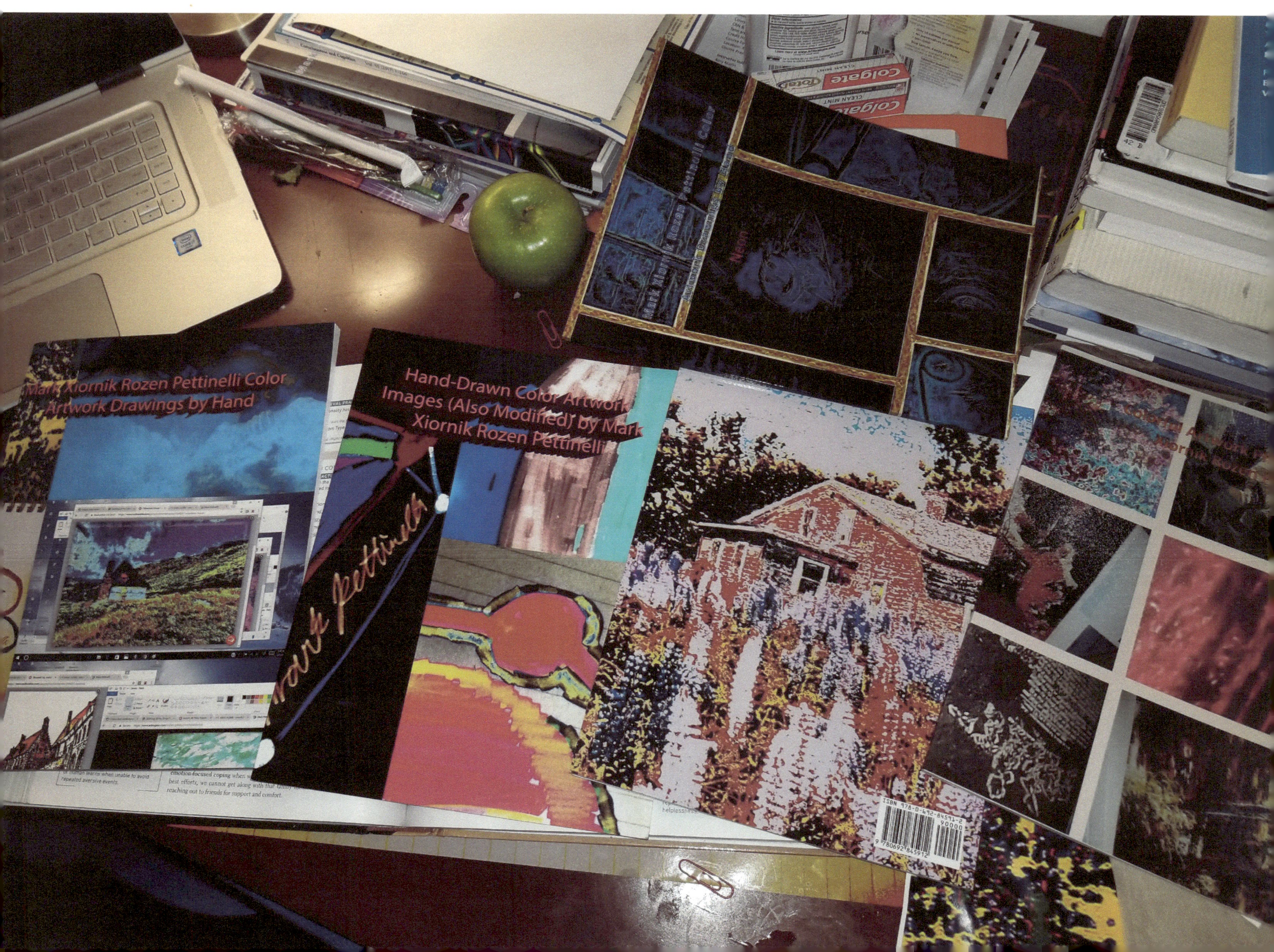

Mark Xiornik Rozen Pettinelli Color
Artwork Drawings by Hand
Hand-Drawn Color Artwork
Images (Also Modified) by Mark
Xiornik Rozen Pettinelli
mark pettinelli
Mark Xiornik Rozen Pettinelli Color
Neon
Colgate
Colgate

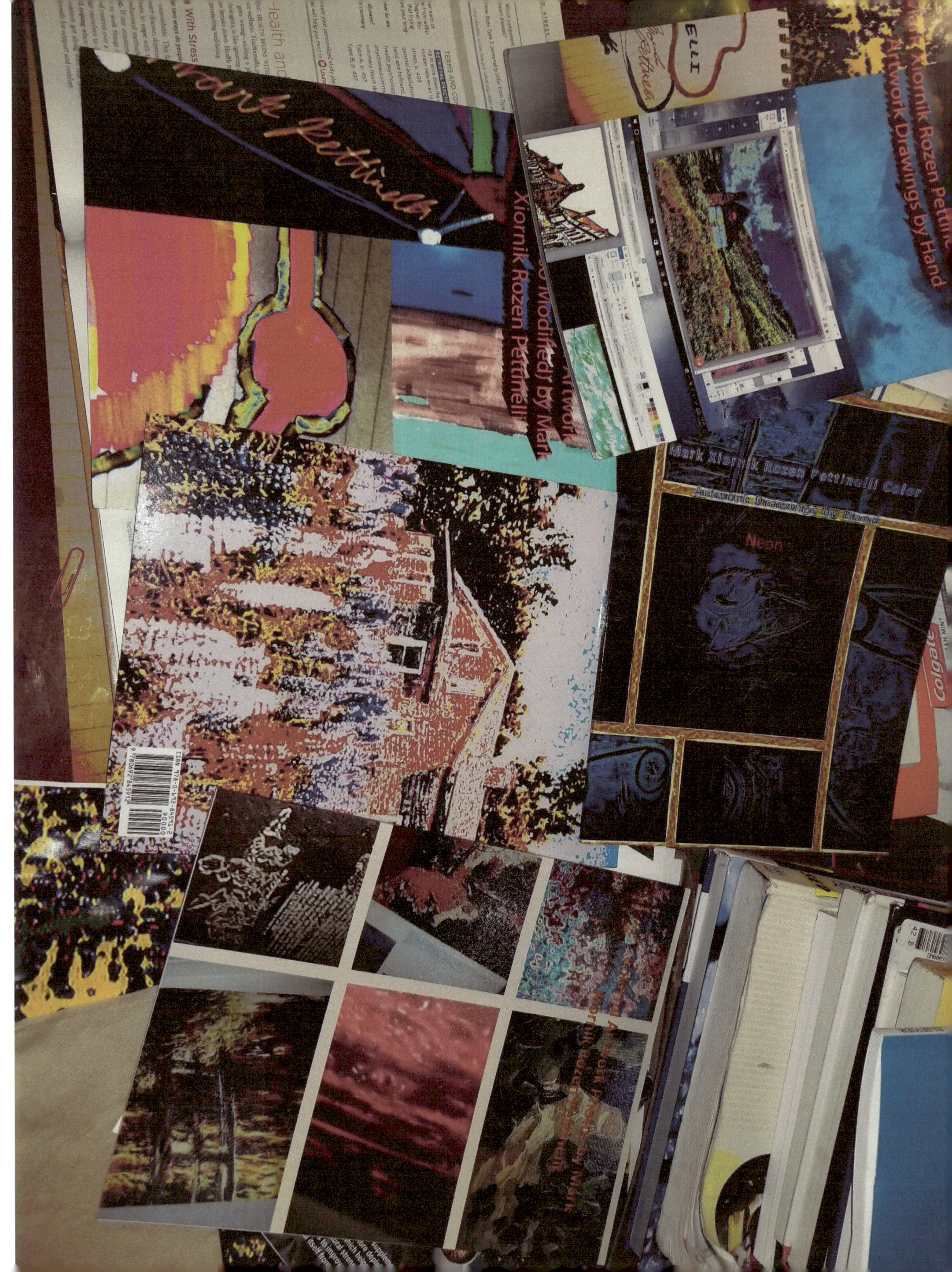

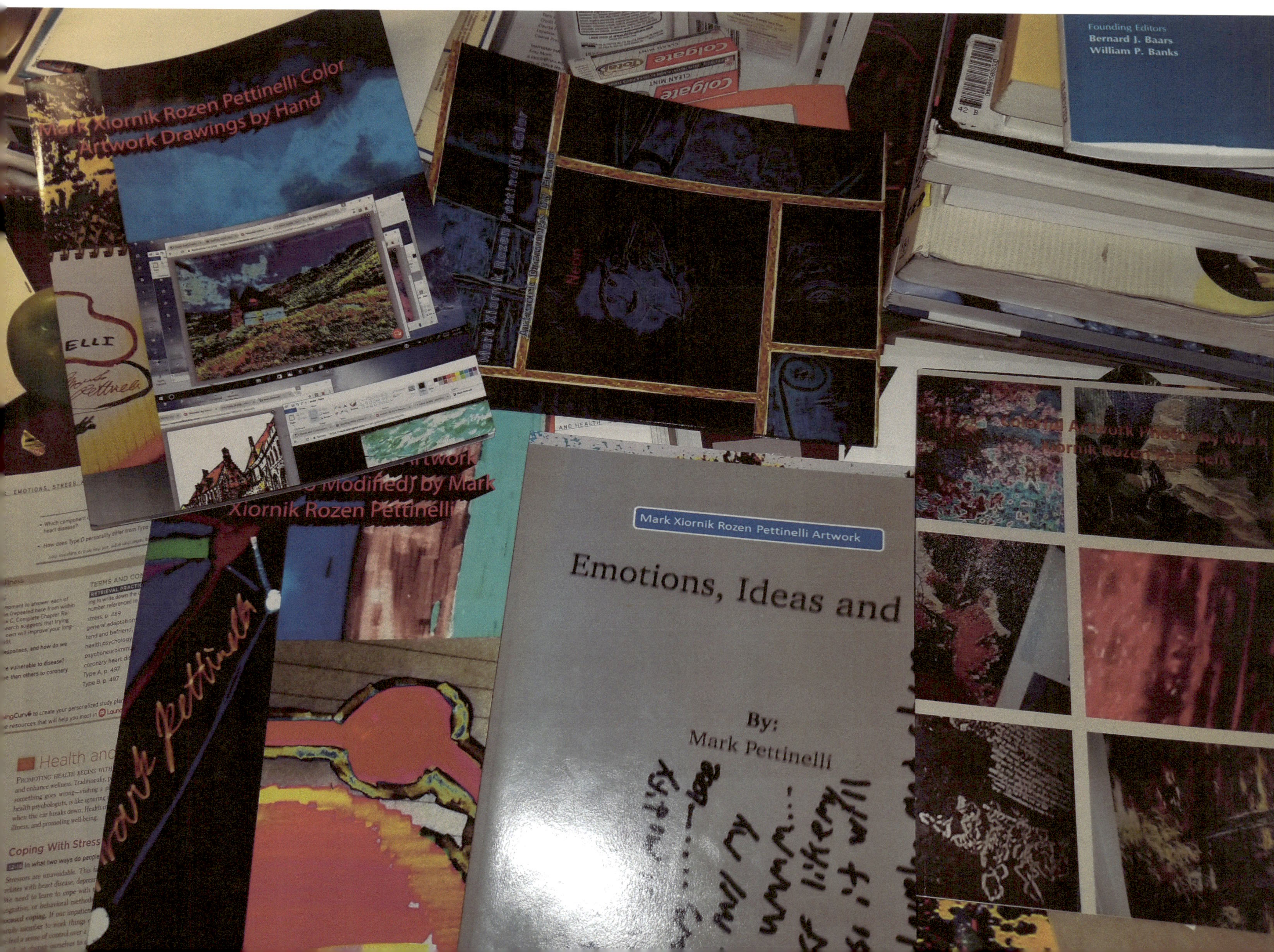
Mark Xiornik Rozen Pettinelli Color
Artwork Drawings by Hand
Neon
Mark Xiornik Rozen Pettinelli Color
Artwork Drawings by Hand
Artwork
Modified by Mark
Xiornik Rozen Pettinelli
Mark Xiornik Rozen Pettinelli Artwork
Emotions, Ideas and
By:
Mark Pettinelli
Founding Editors
Bernard J. Baars
William P. Banks
Colgate
Health and
Coping With Stress

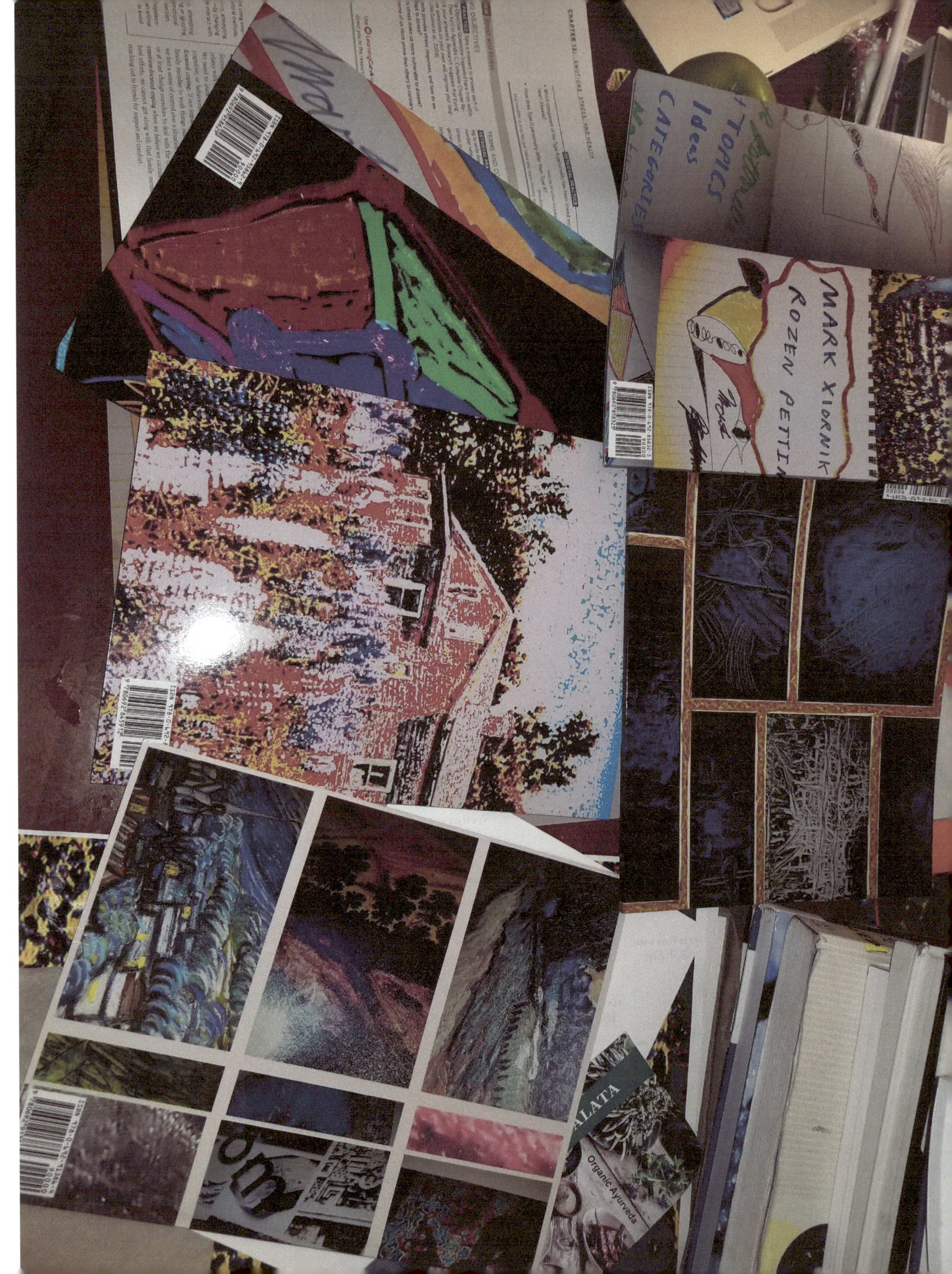

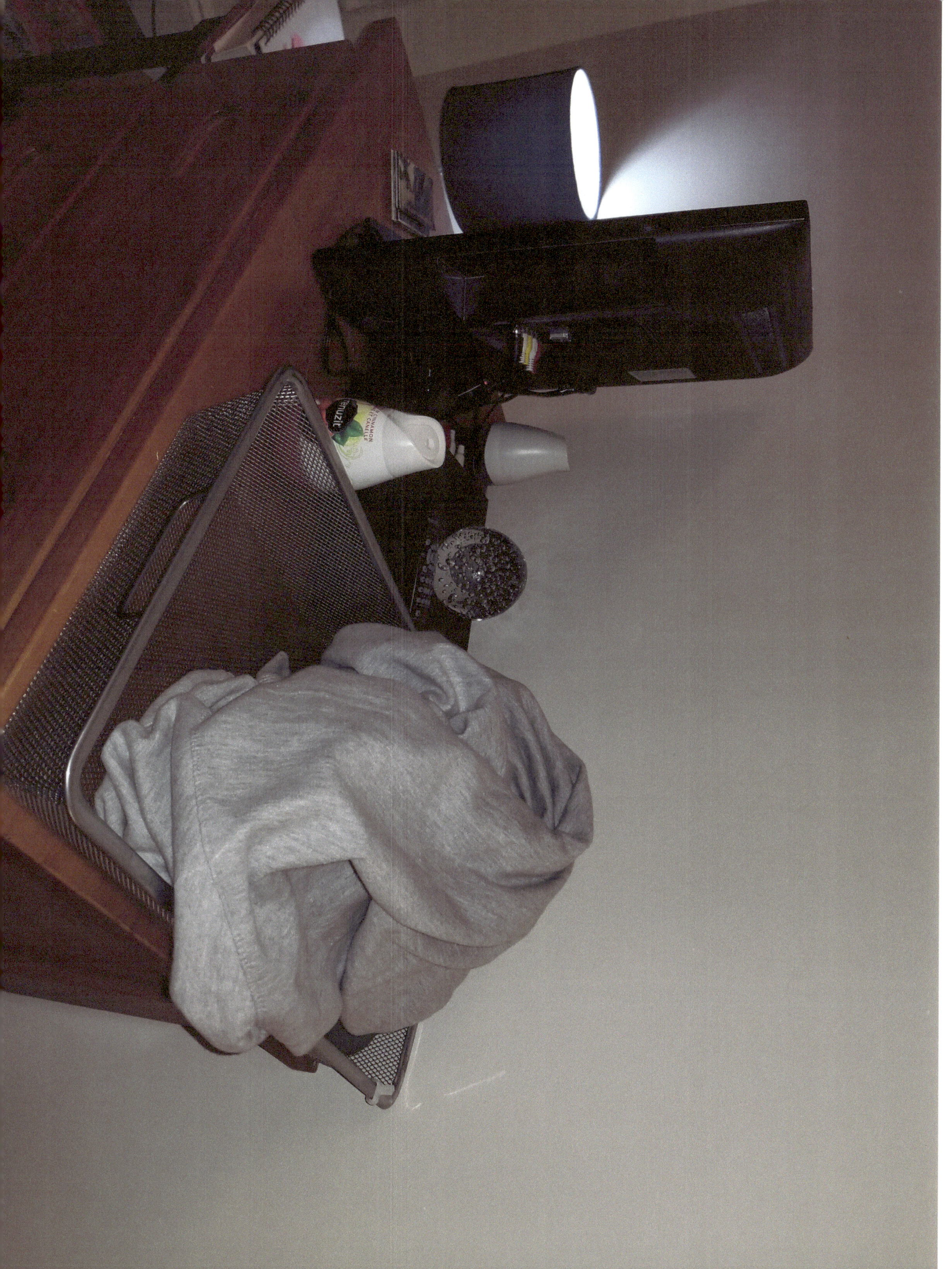

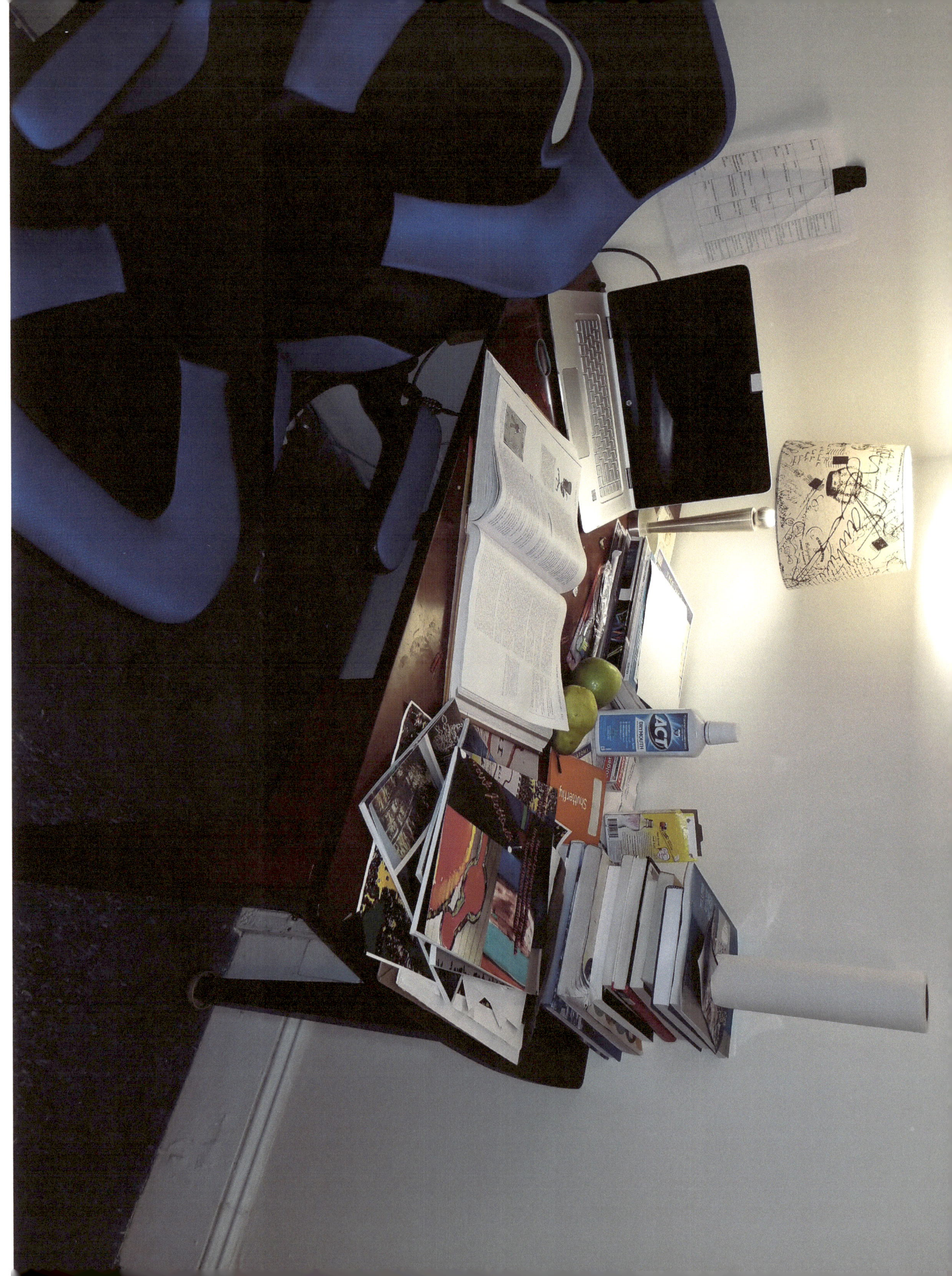

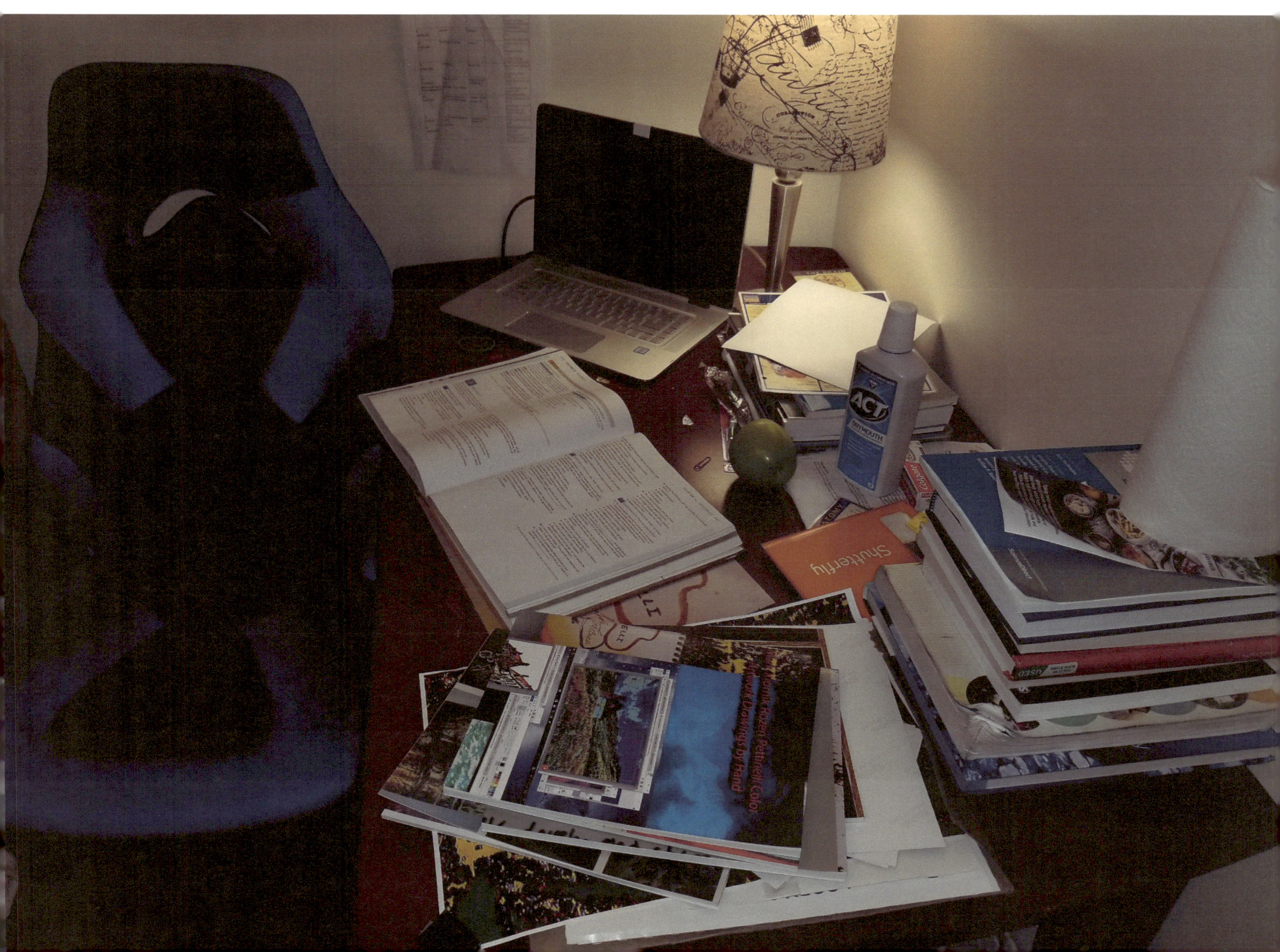

ACT
Shutterfly

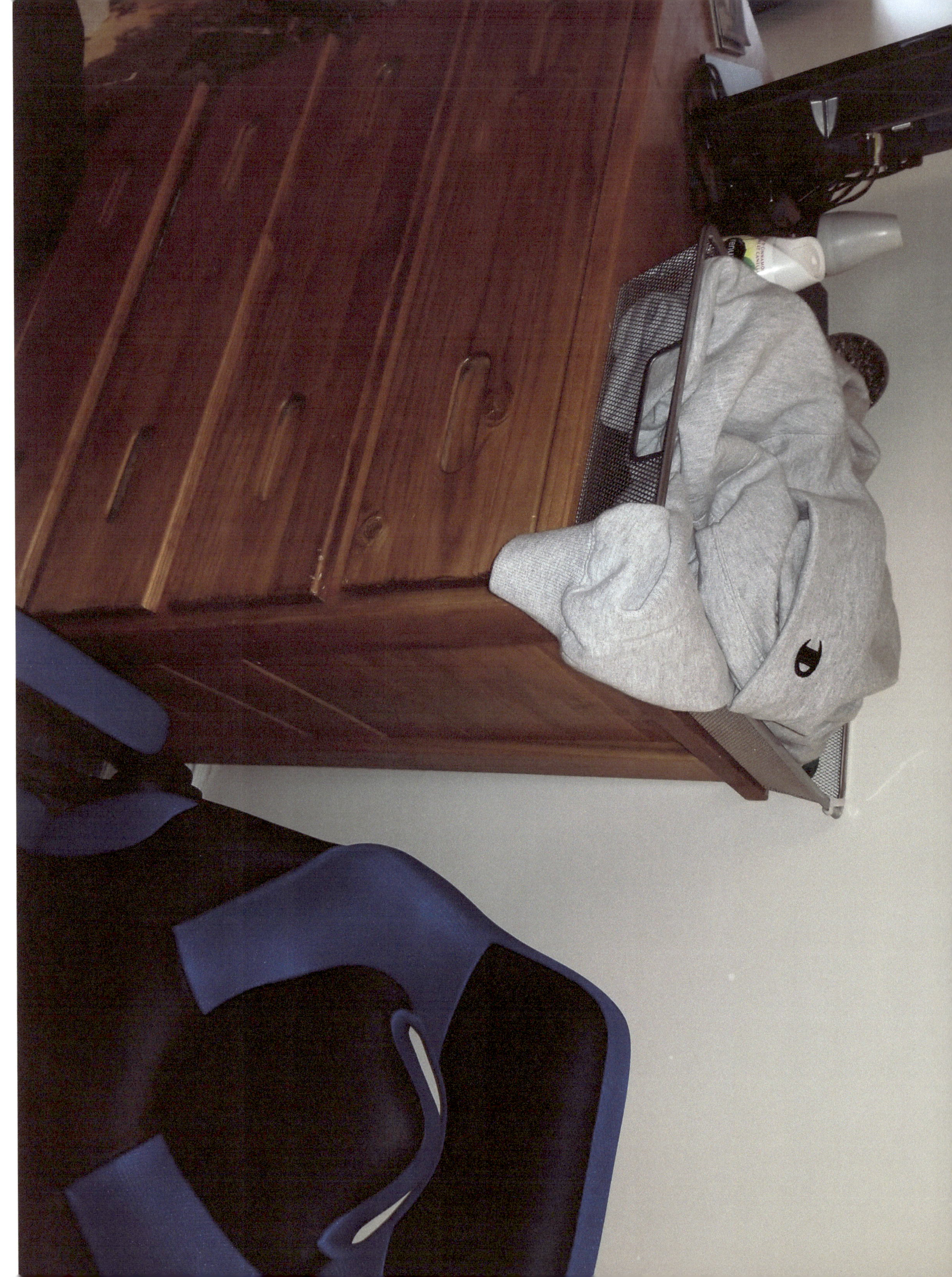

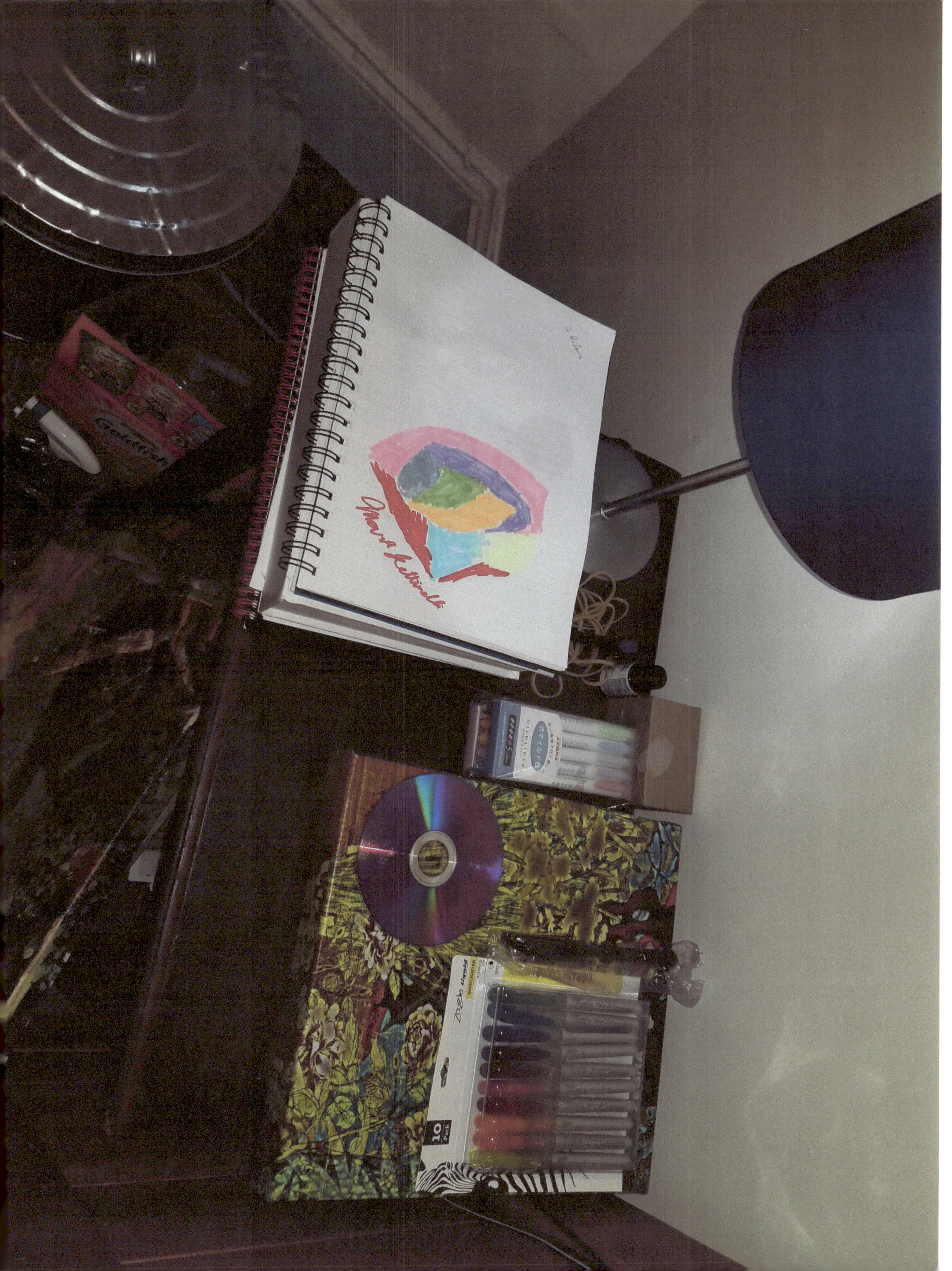

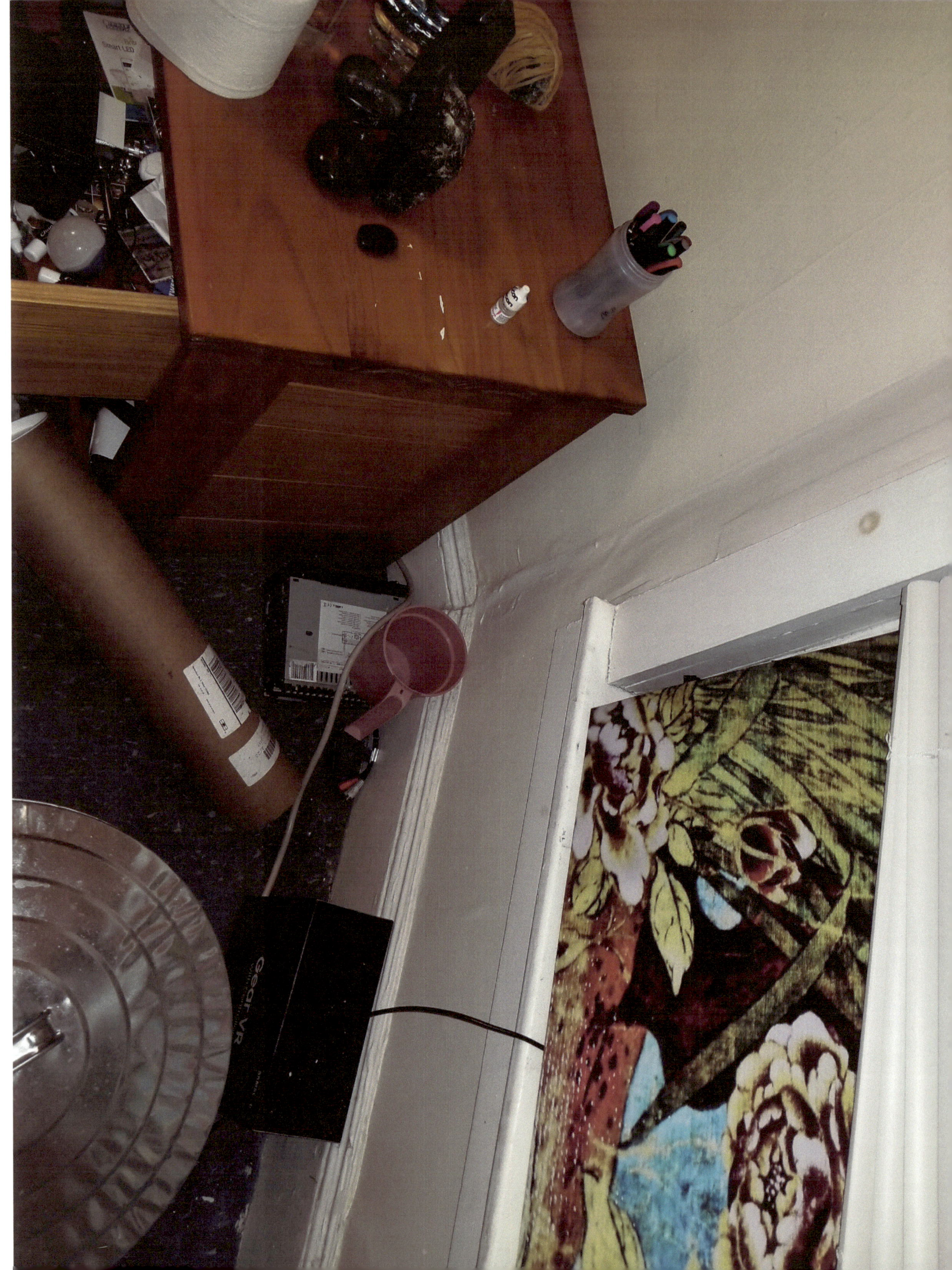

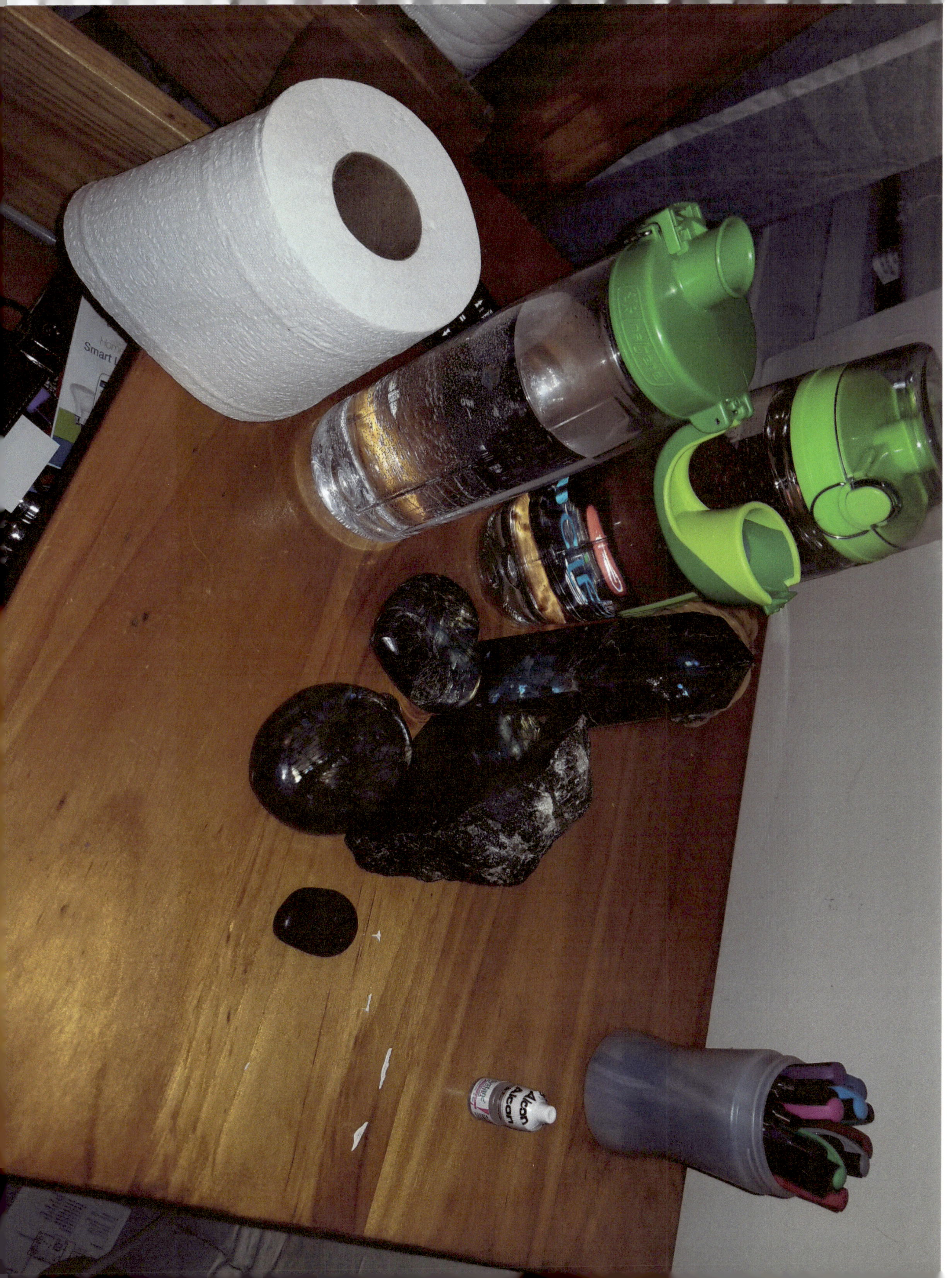

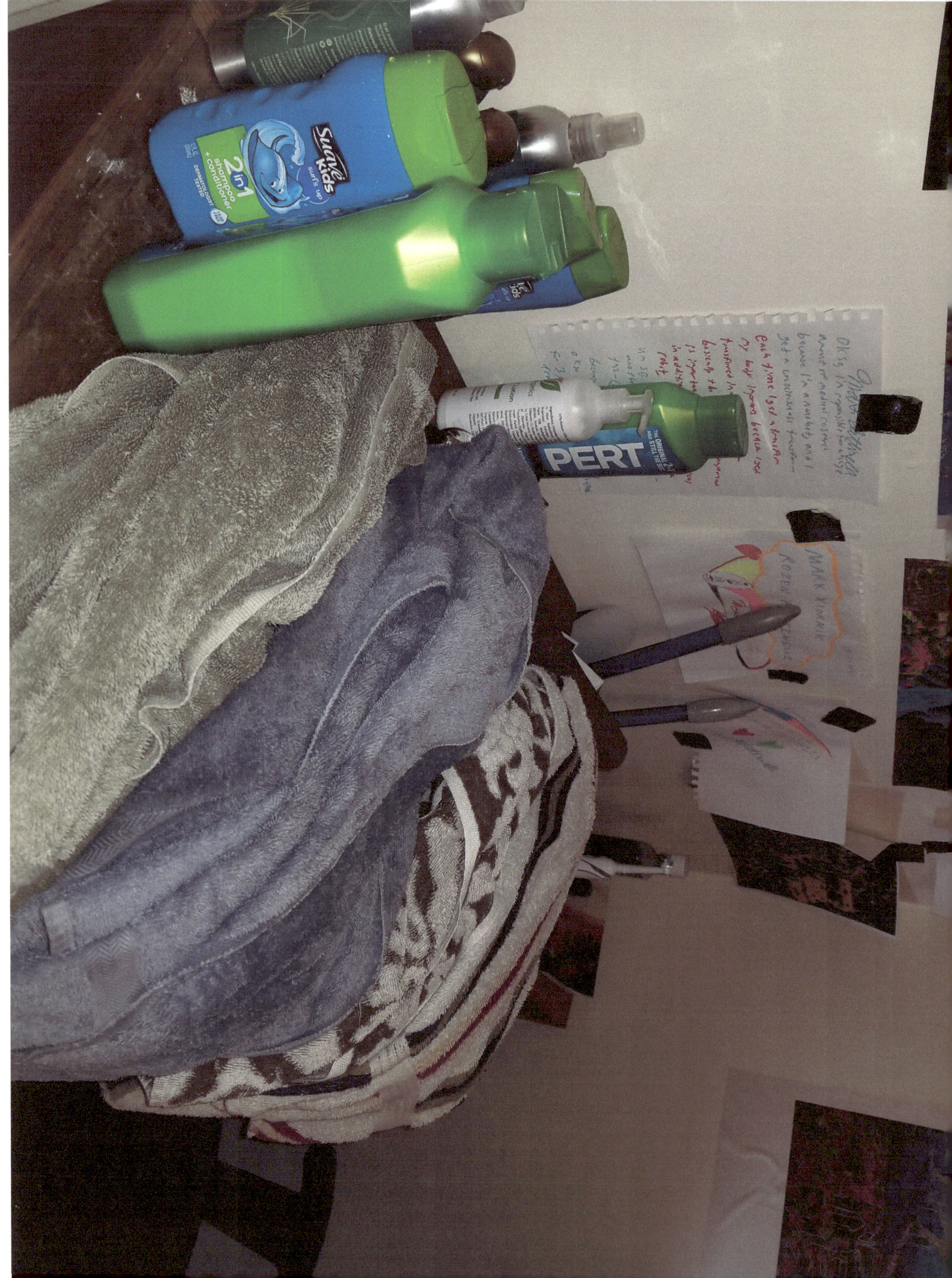

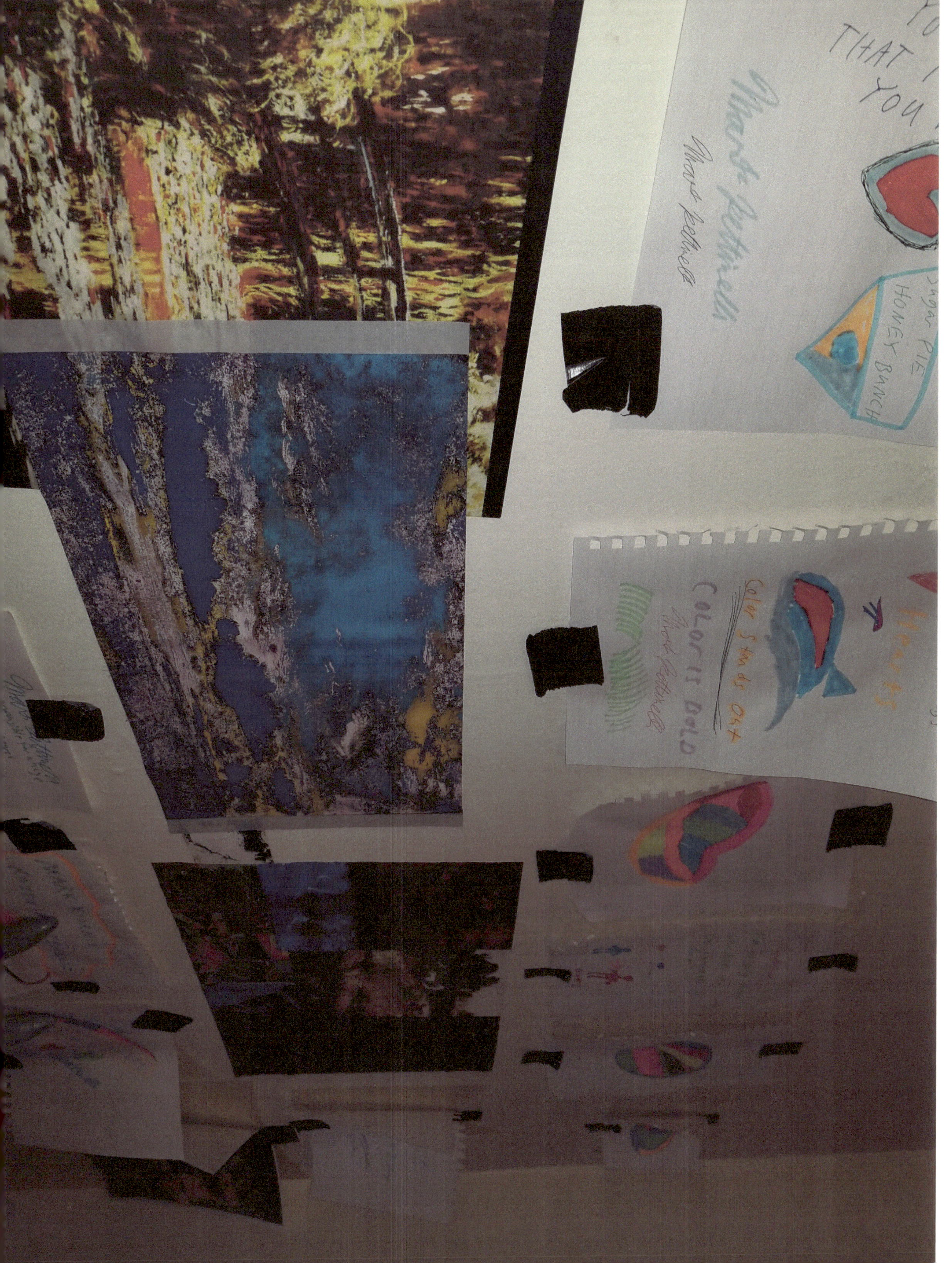
THAT YOU
YOU
Marta Pettinella
Sugar PIE
HONEY BUNCH
Color Stands Out
COLOR IS BOLD
Marta Pettinella
HEARTS

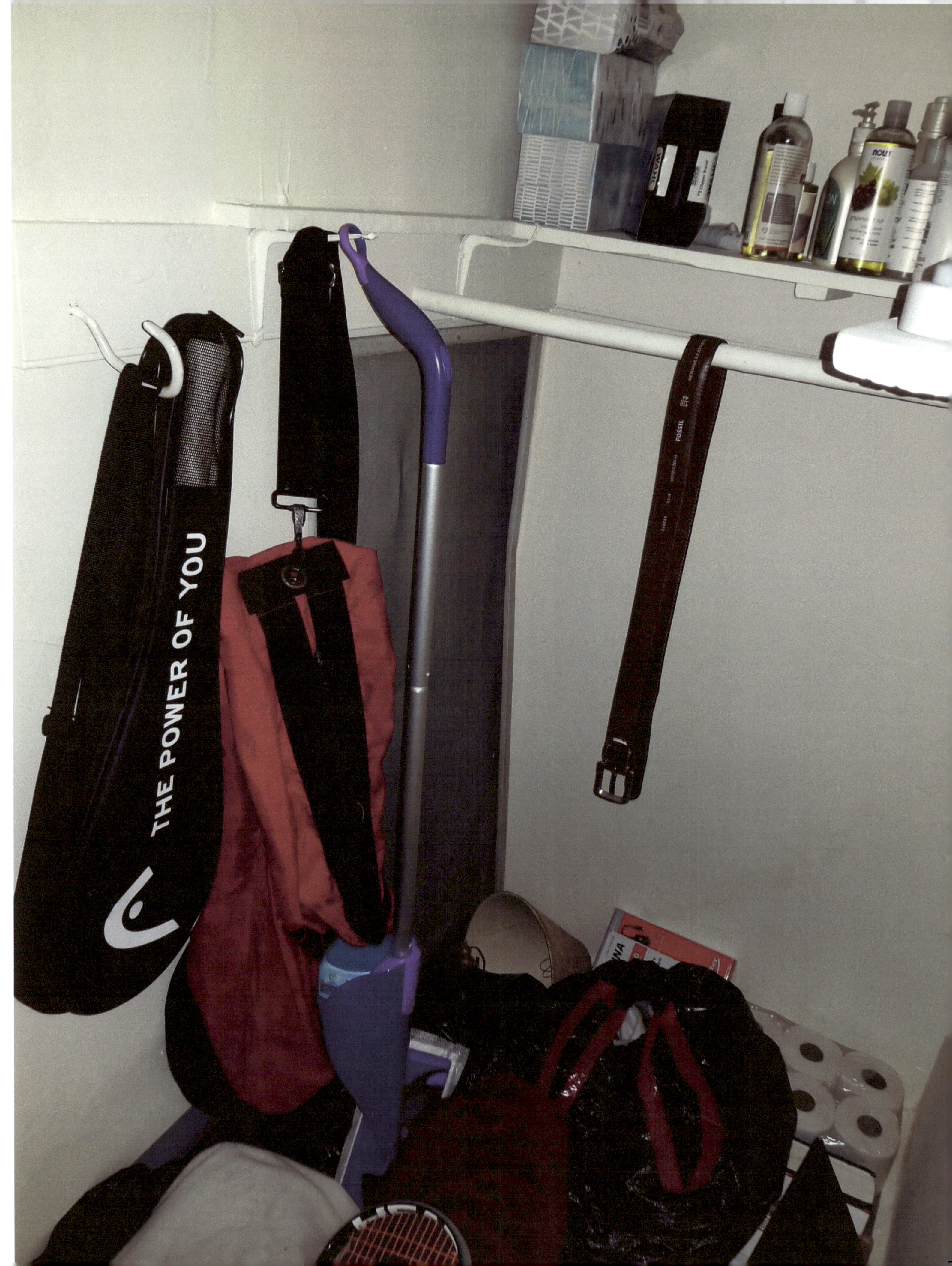

THE POWER OF YOU
FOSSIL
GENUINE LEATHER

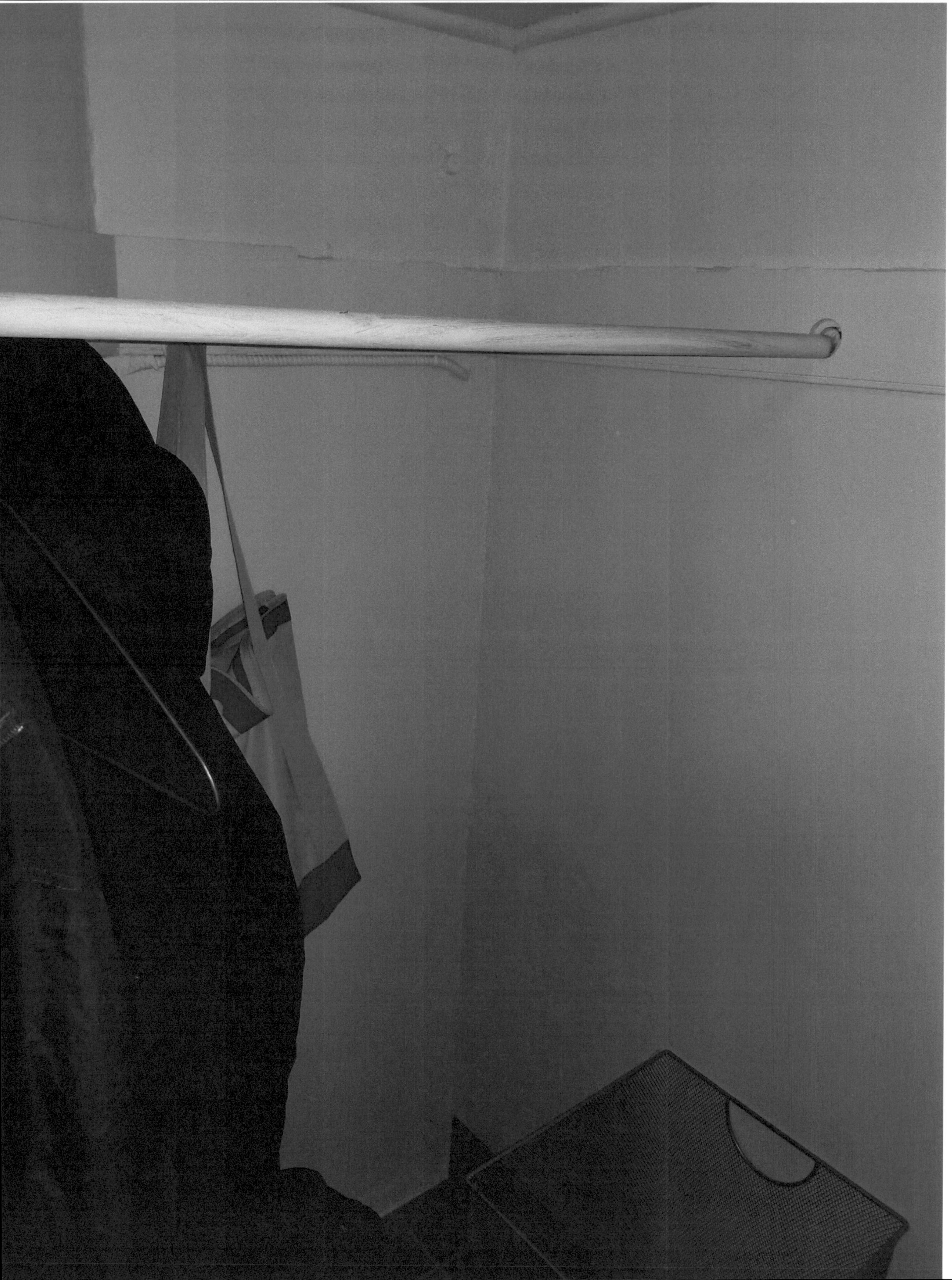

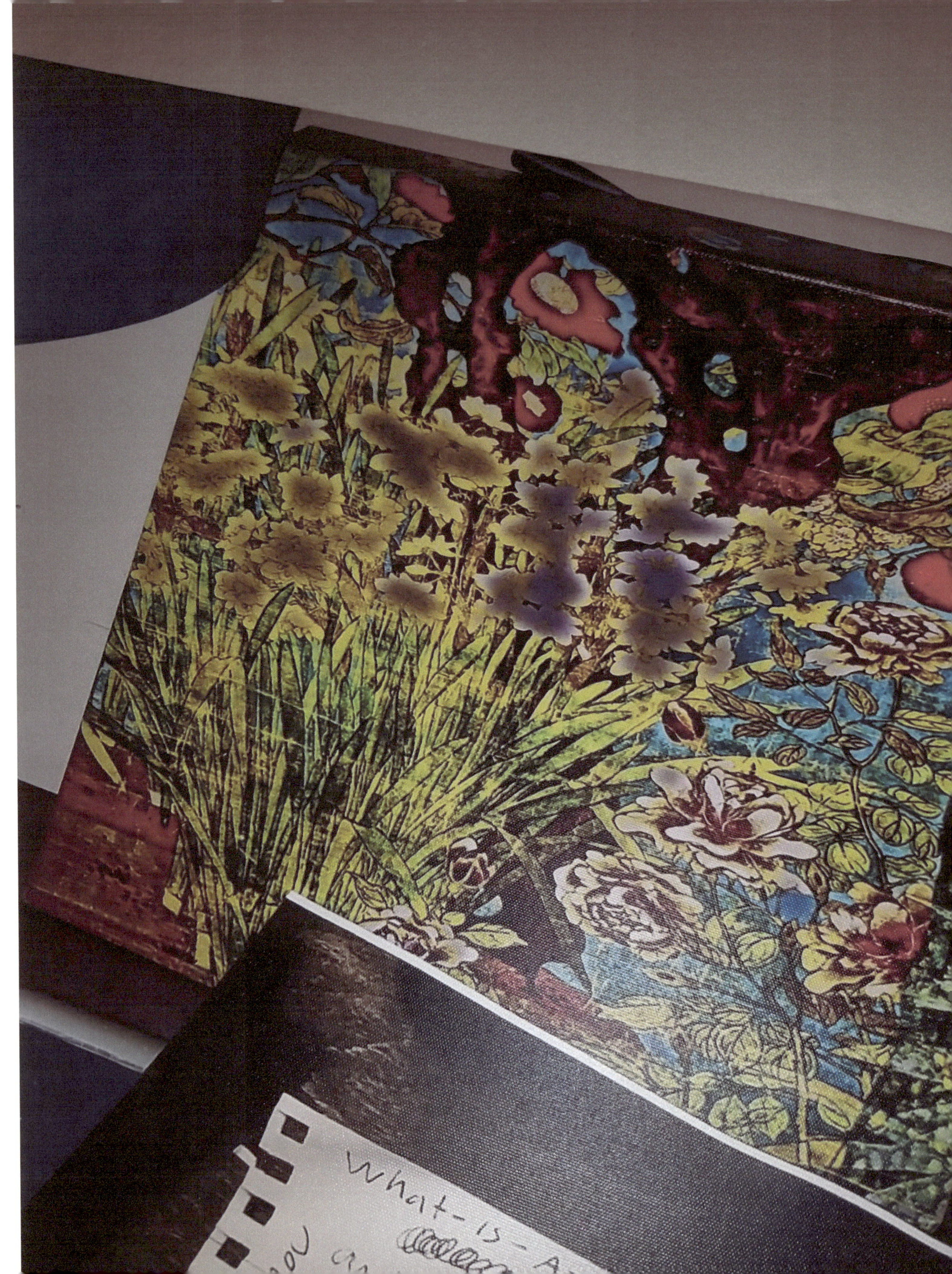
What-is-A

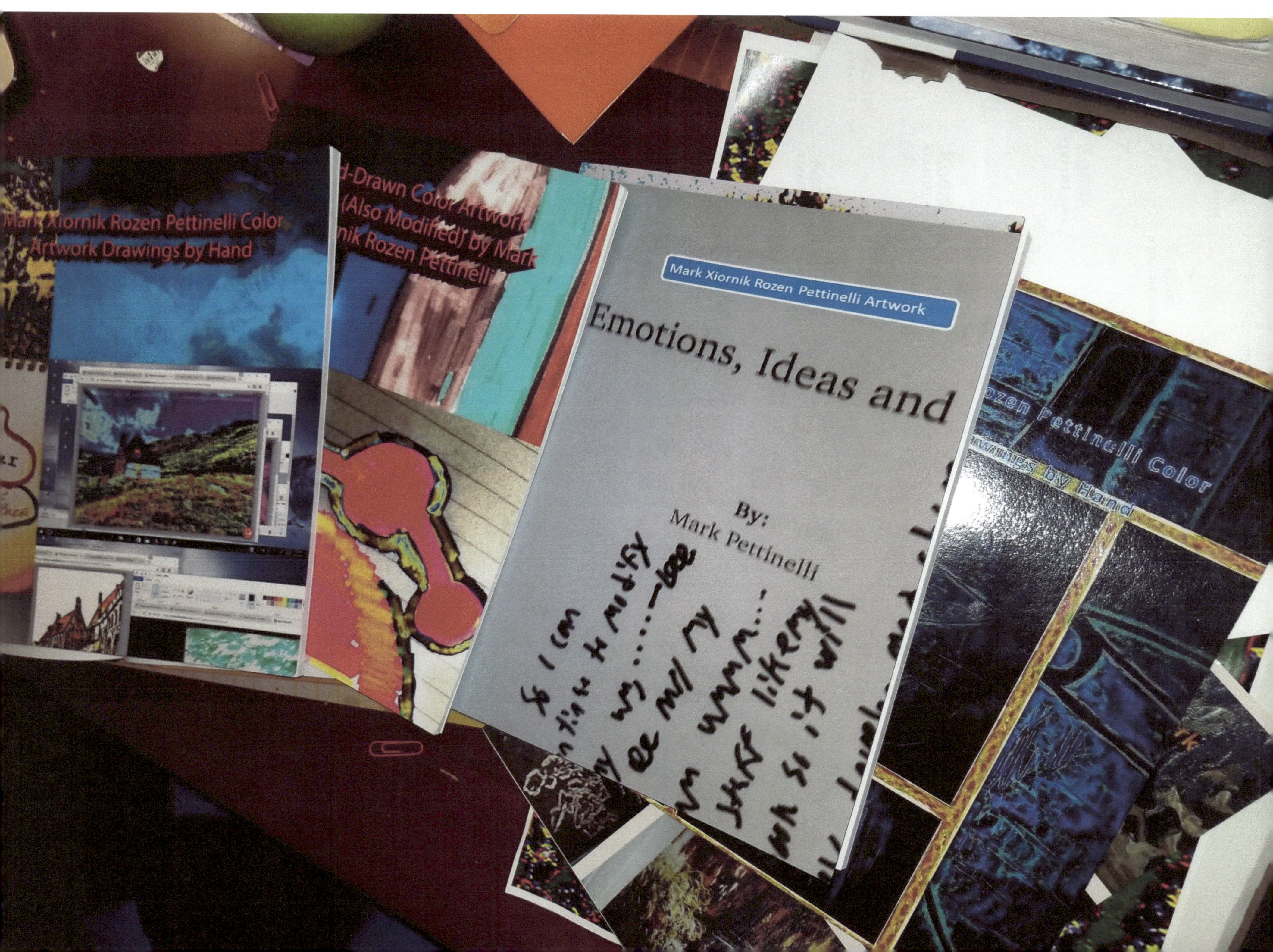
Mark Xiornik Rozen Pettinelli Artwork
Emotions, Ideas and
By:
Mark Pettinelli
Mark Xiornik Rozen Pettinelli Color
Artwork Drawings by Hand
Hand-Drawn Color Artwork
(Also Modified) by Mark
Xiornik Rozen Pettinelli
Rozen Pettinelli Color
Drawings by Hand

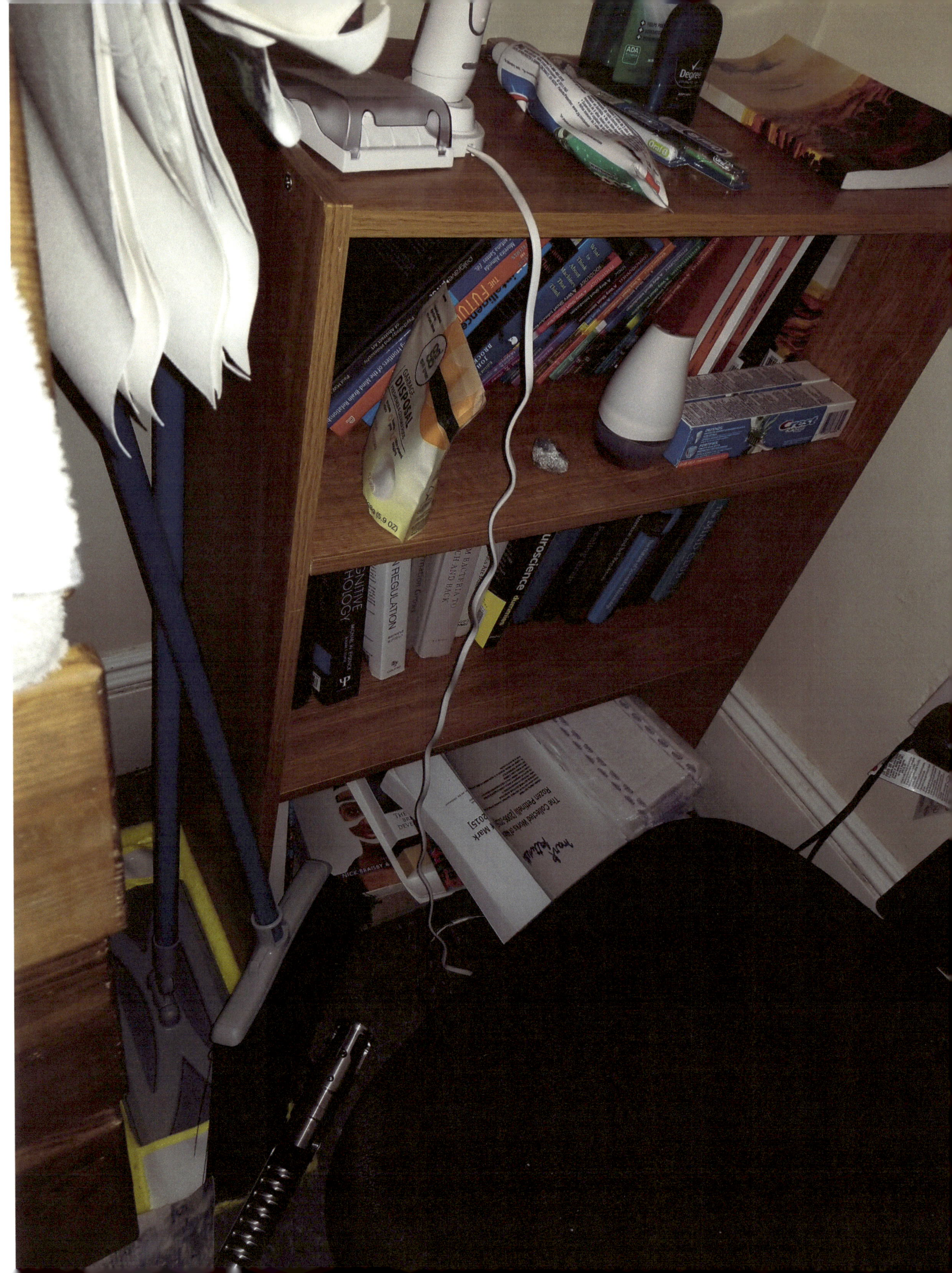

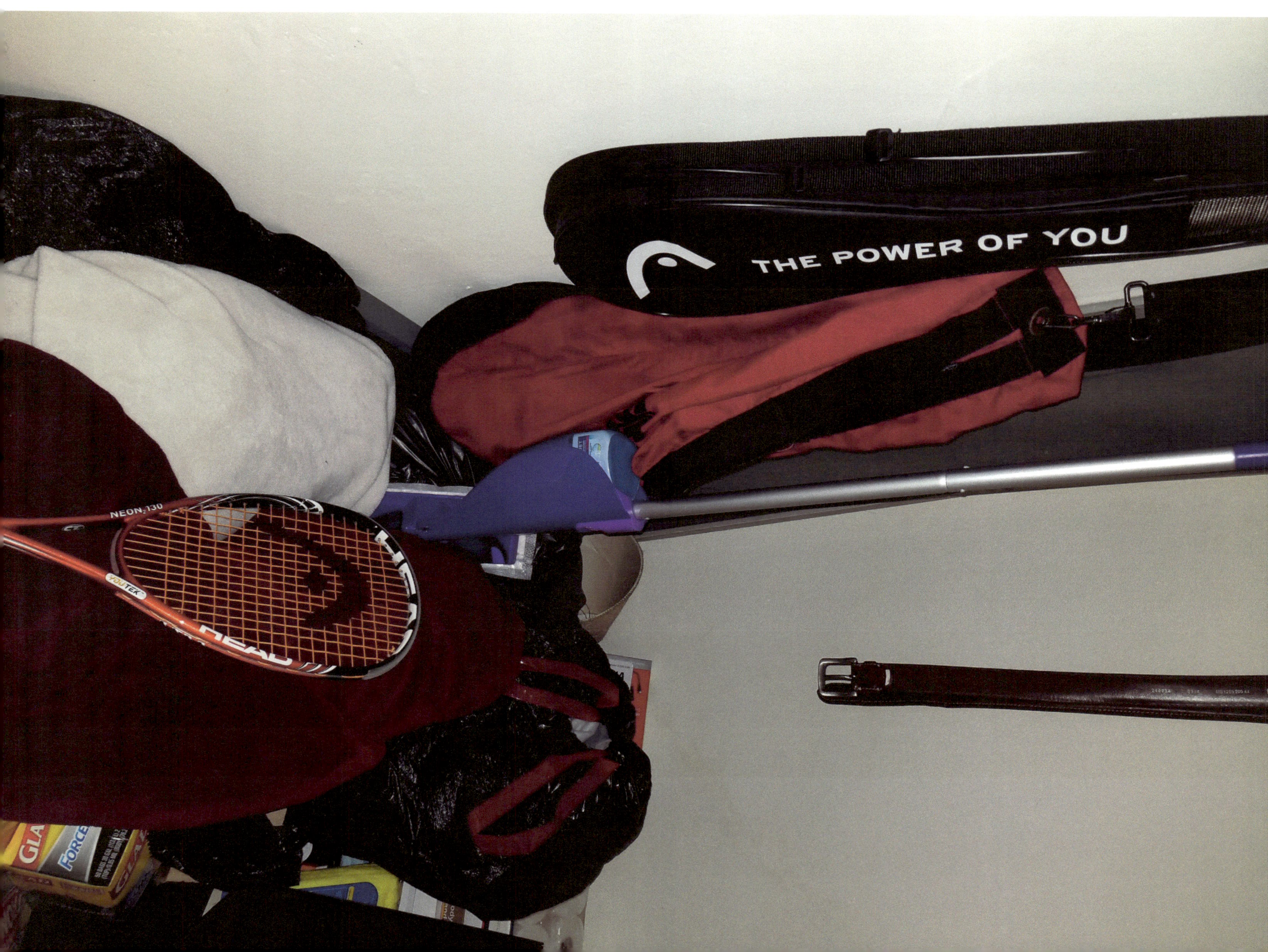

THE POWER OF YOU
HEAD
NEON 130
YOU TEK
GLAD
FORCE

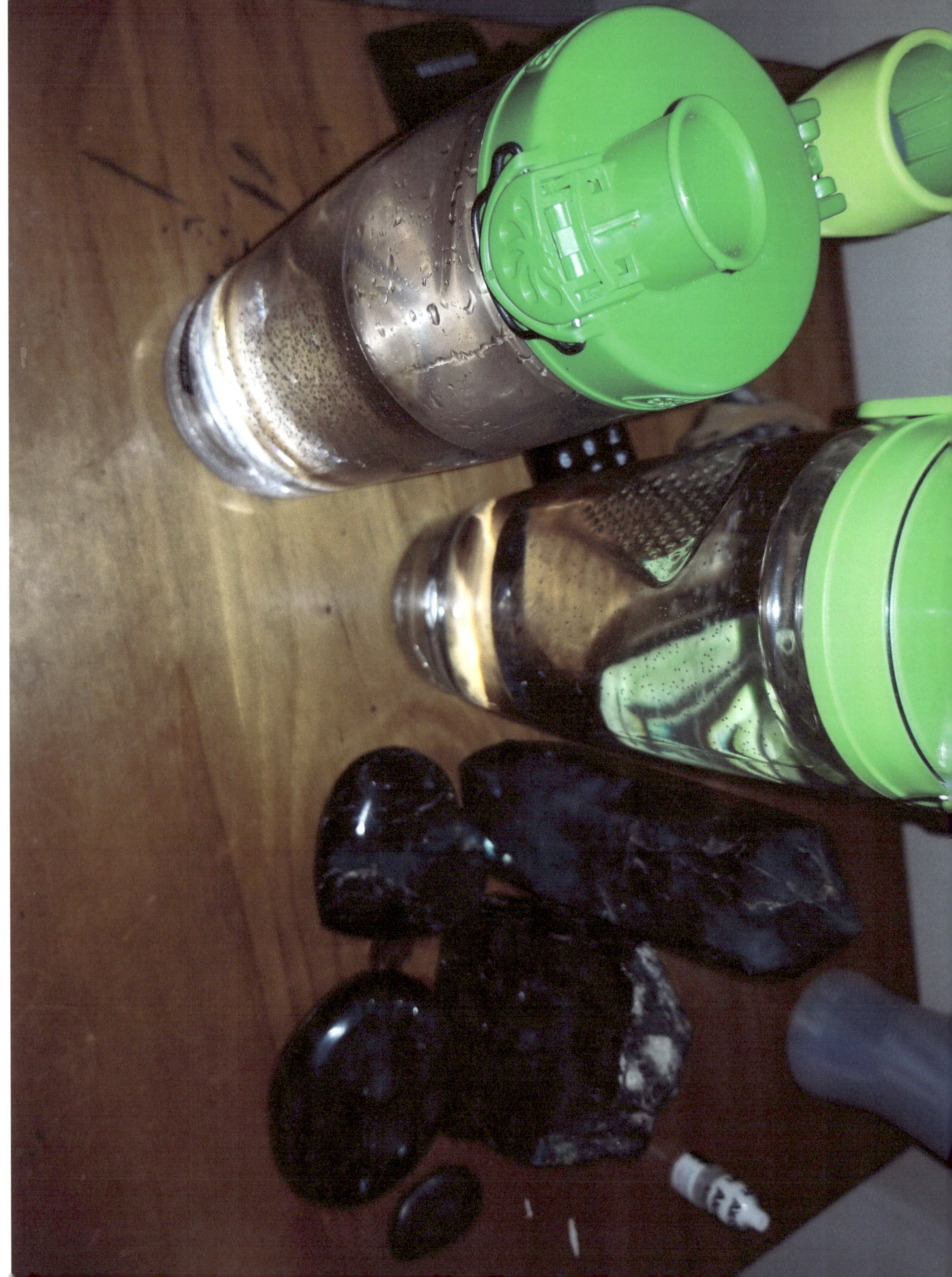

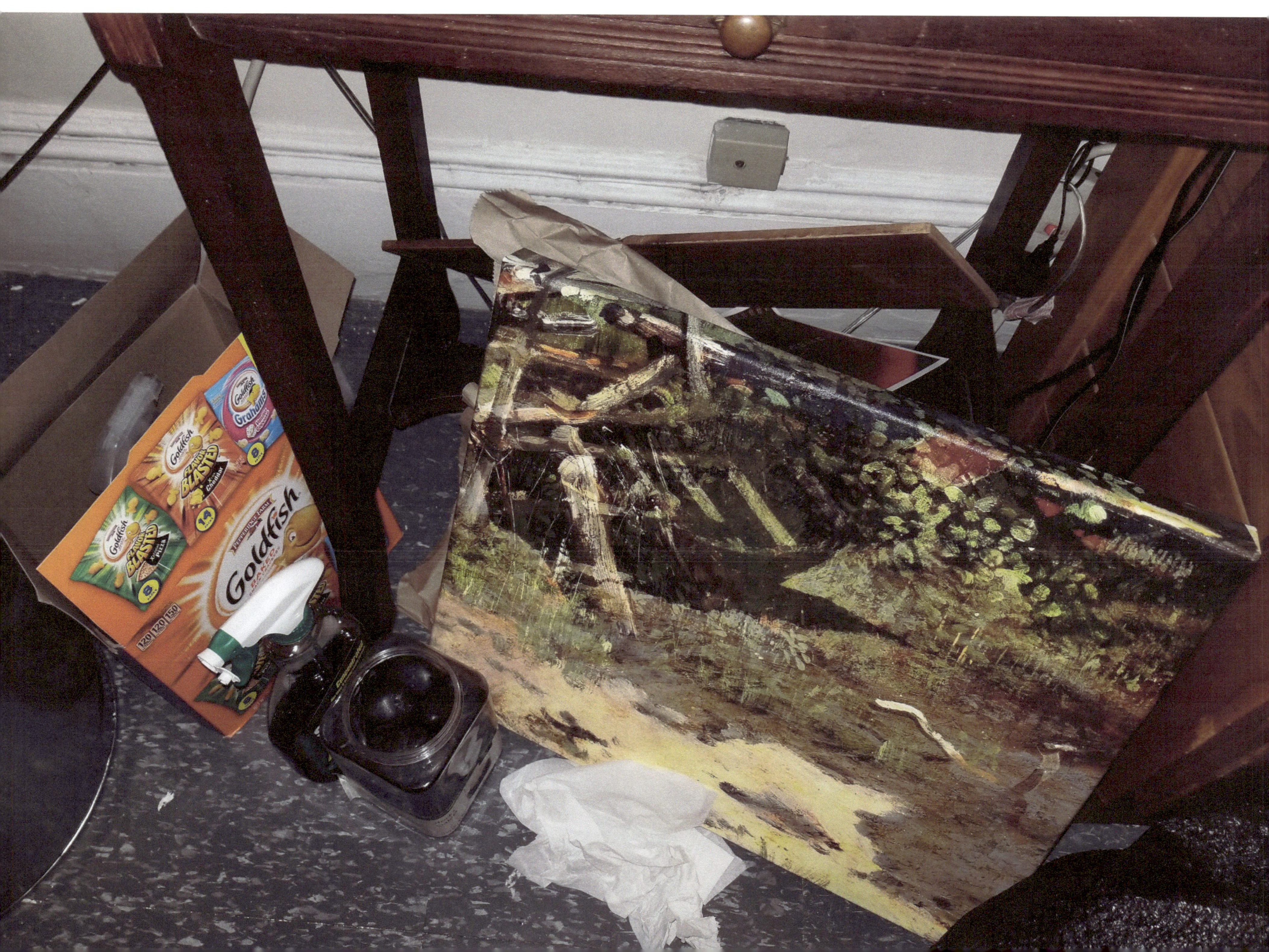
Goldfish
FLAVOR BLASTED
Goldfish
Grahams

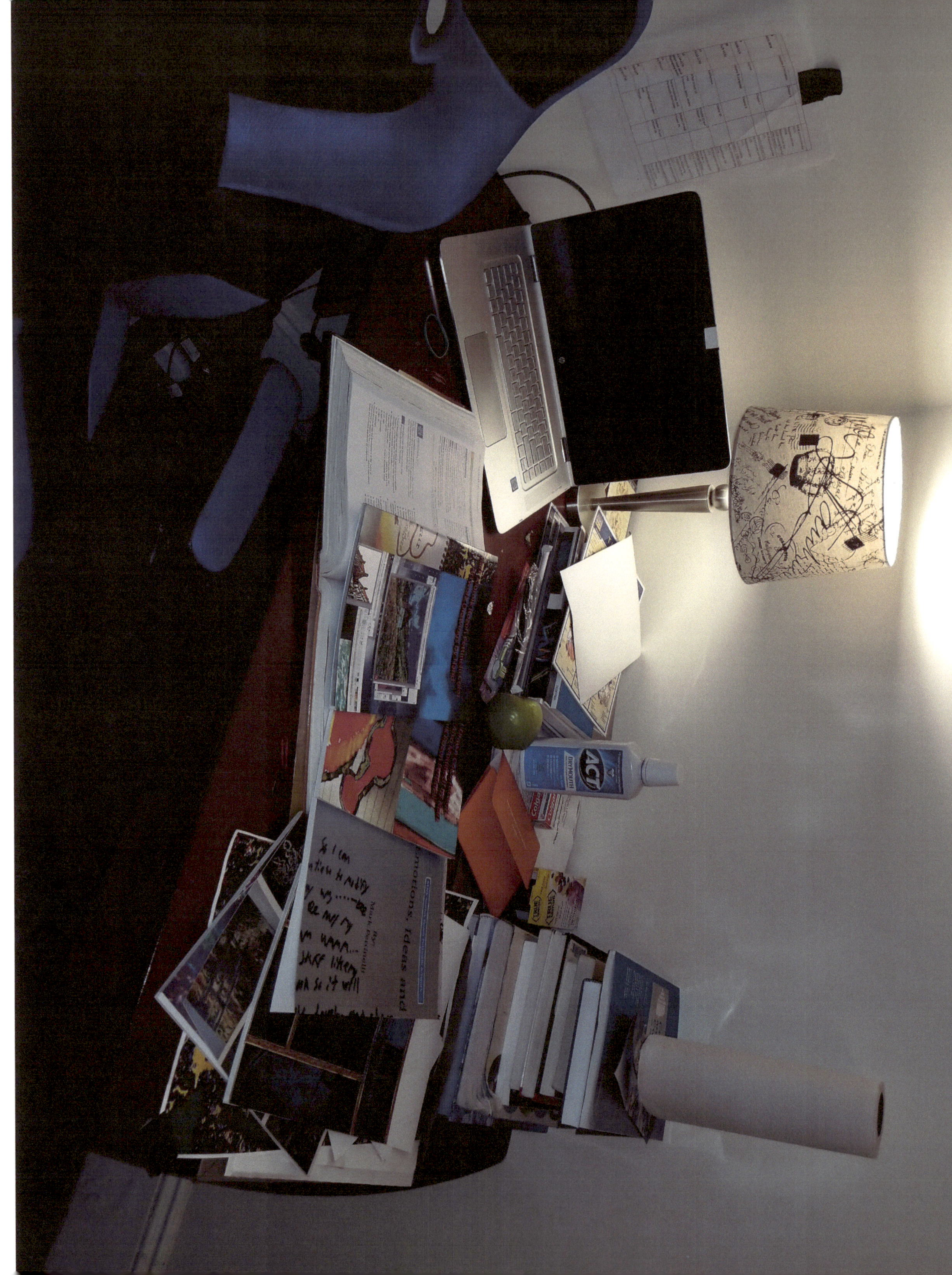

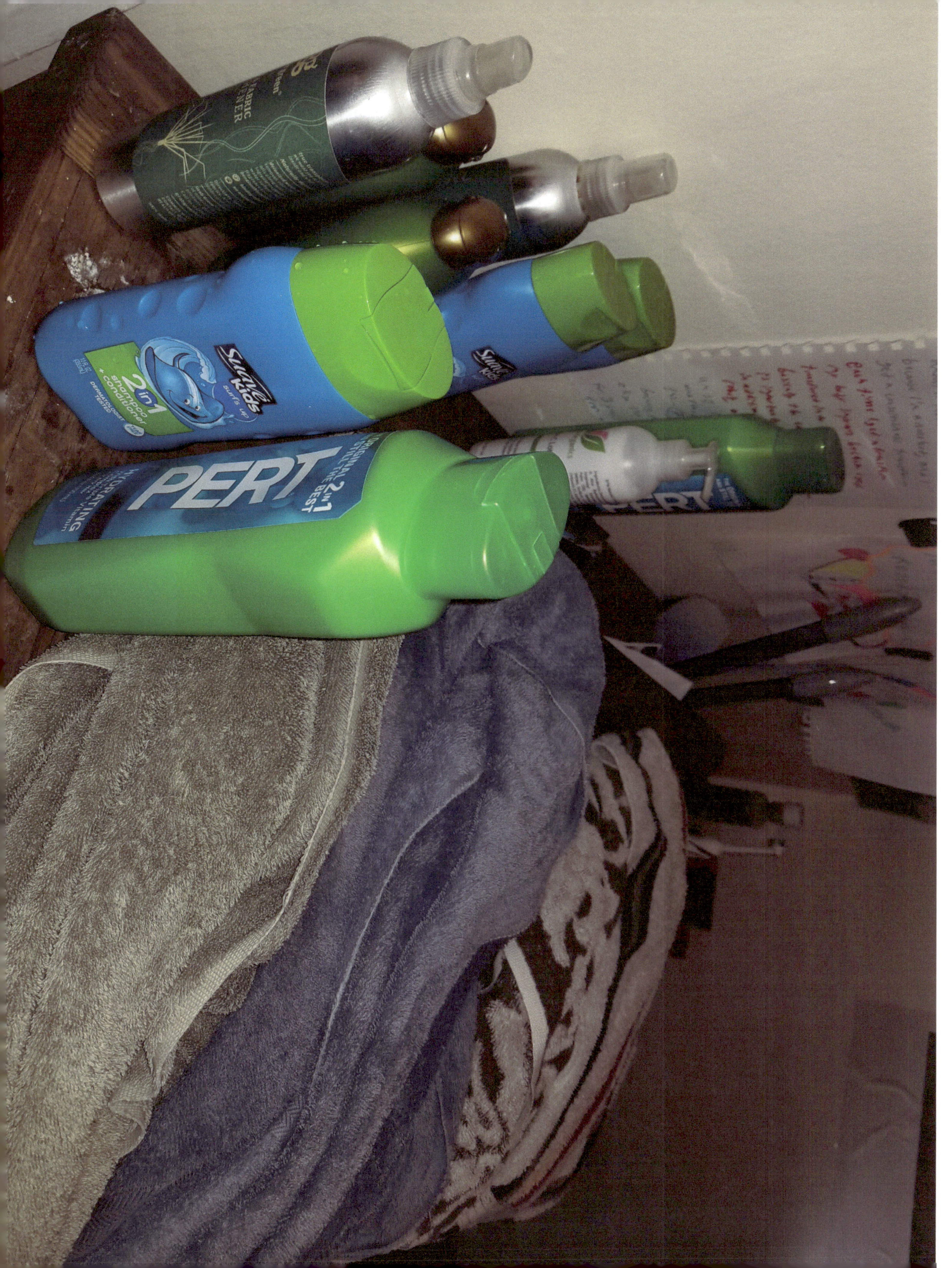

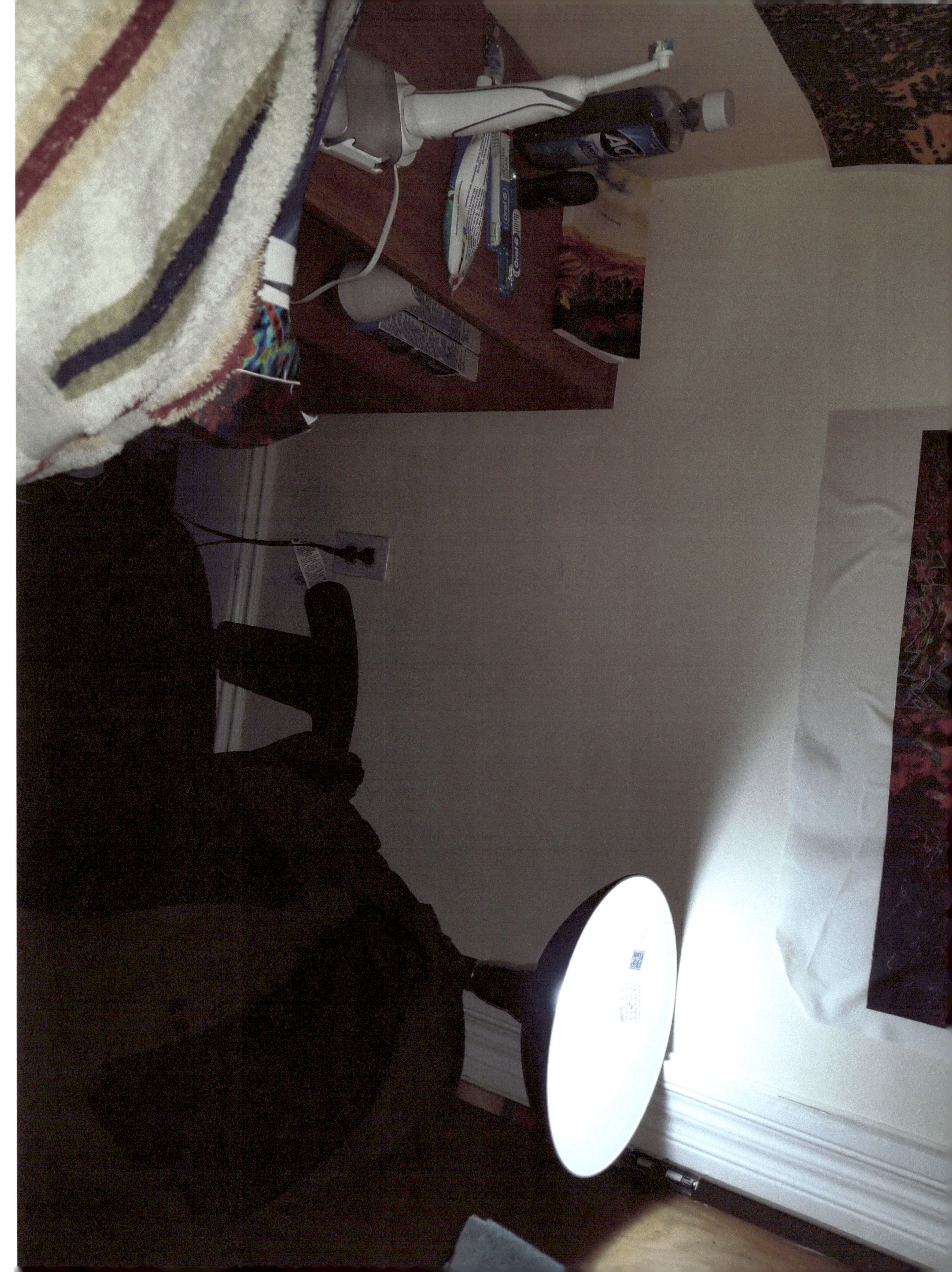

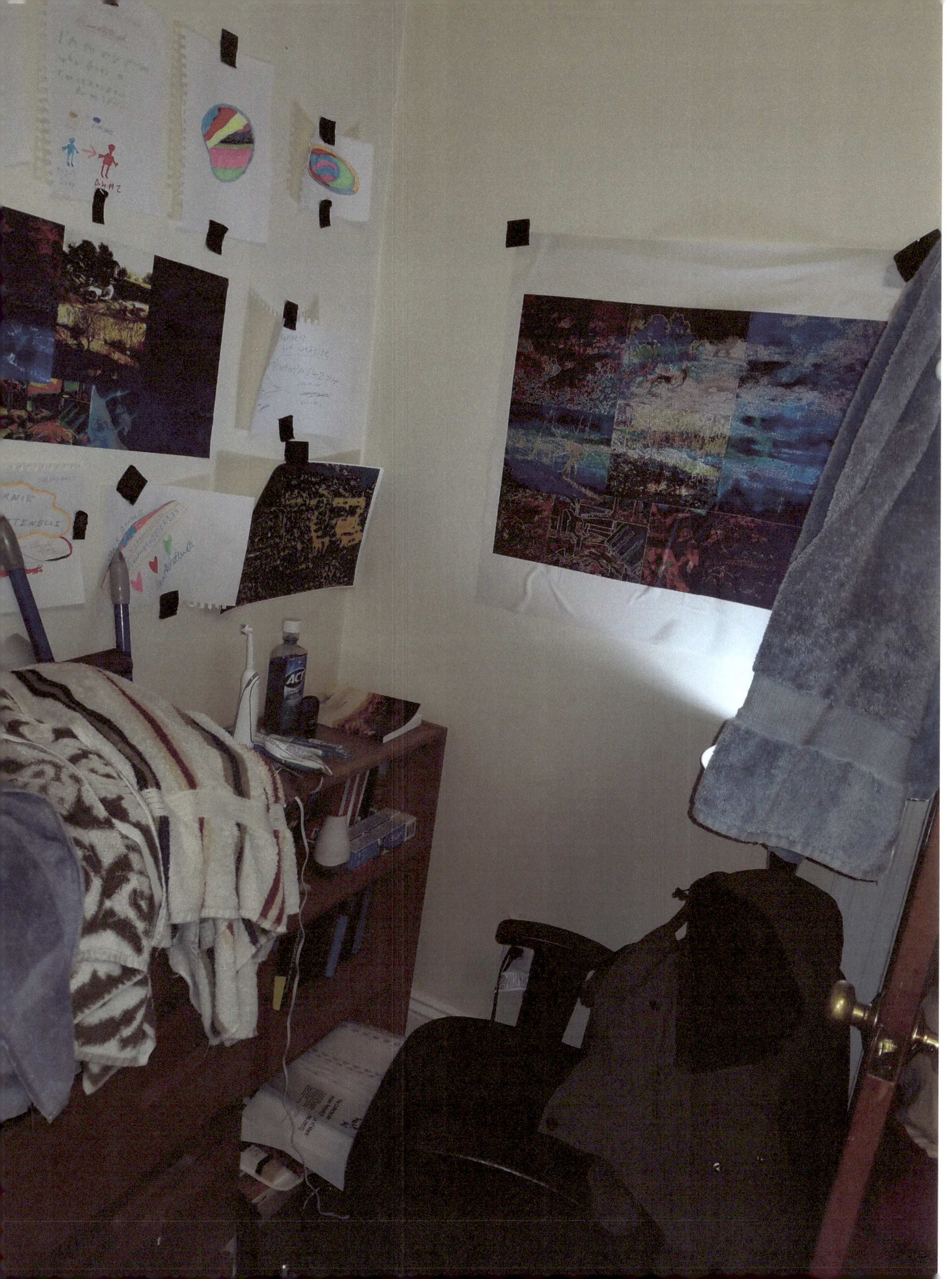

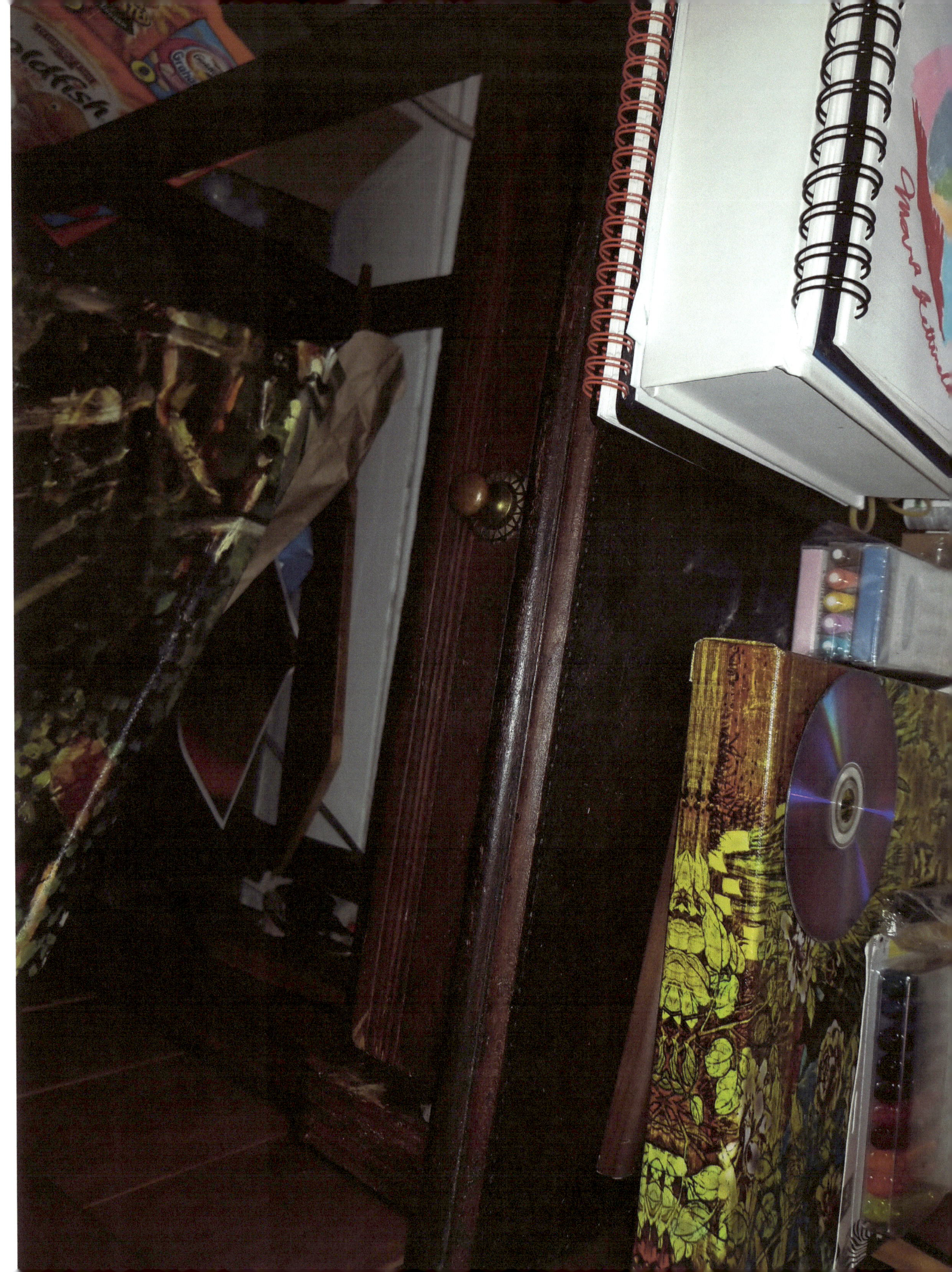

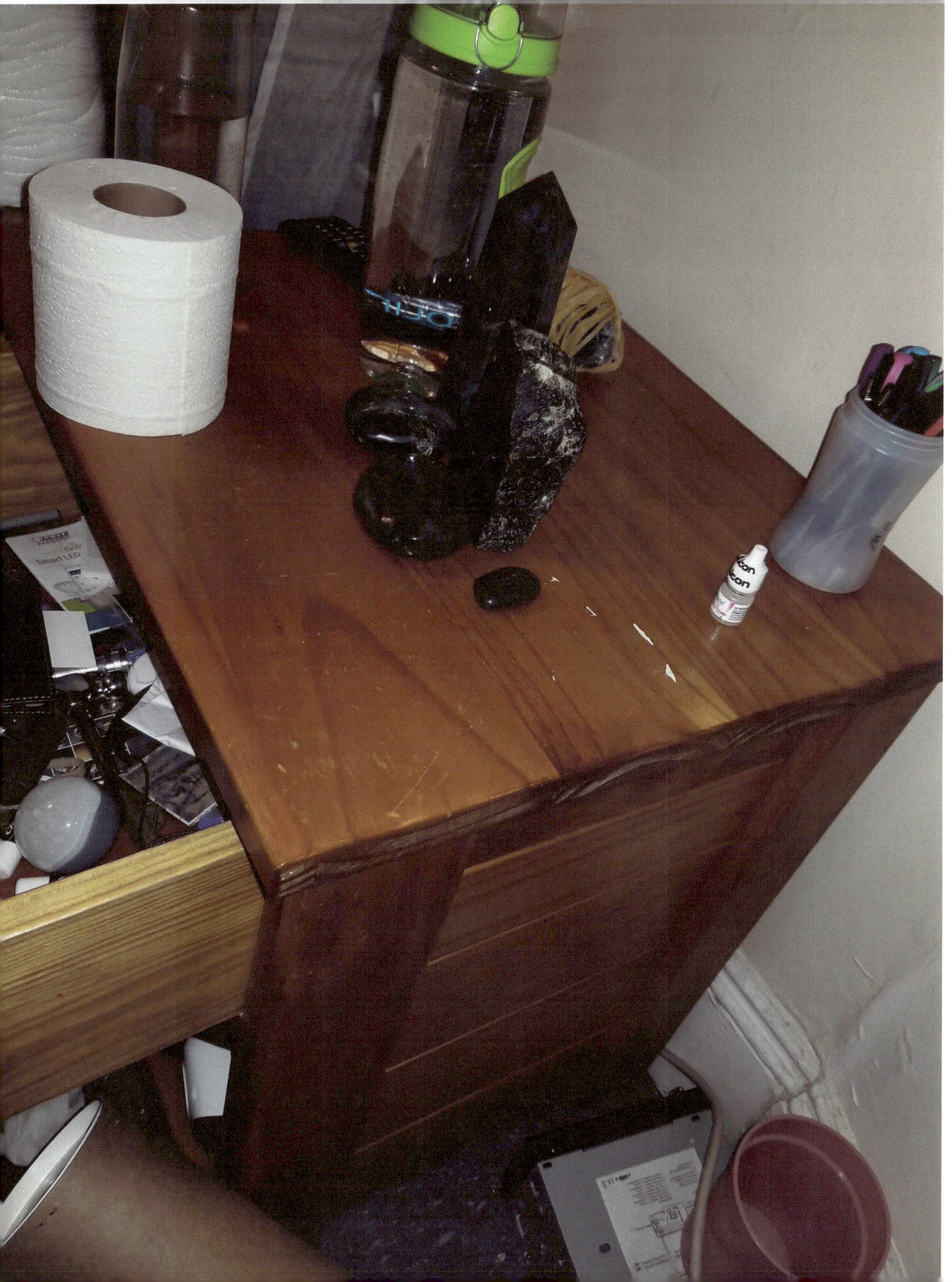

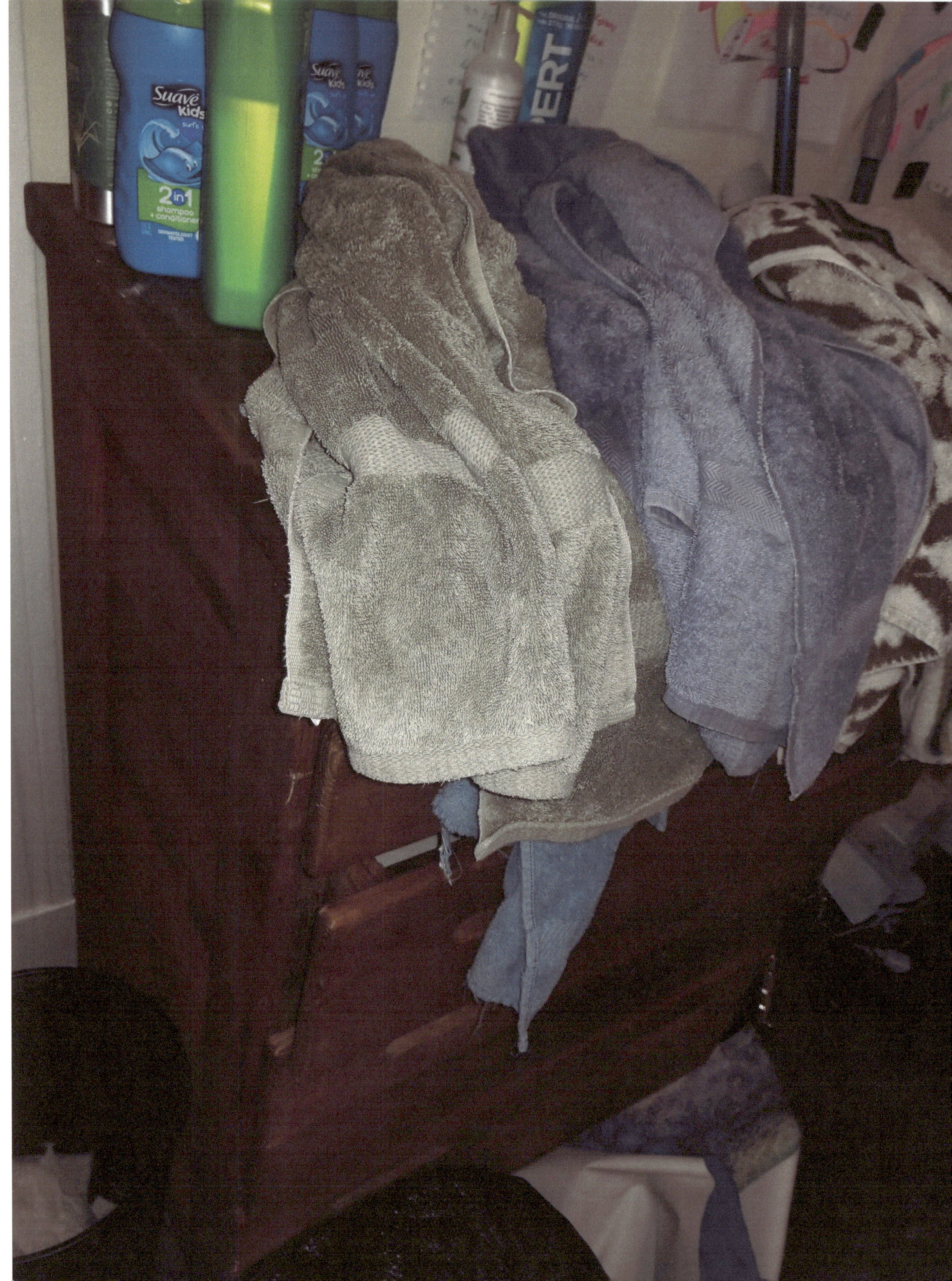

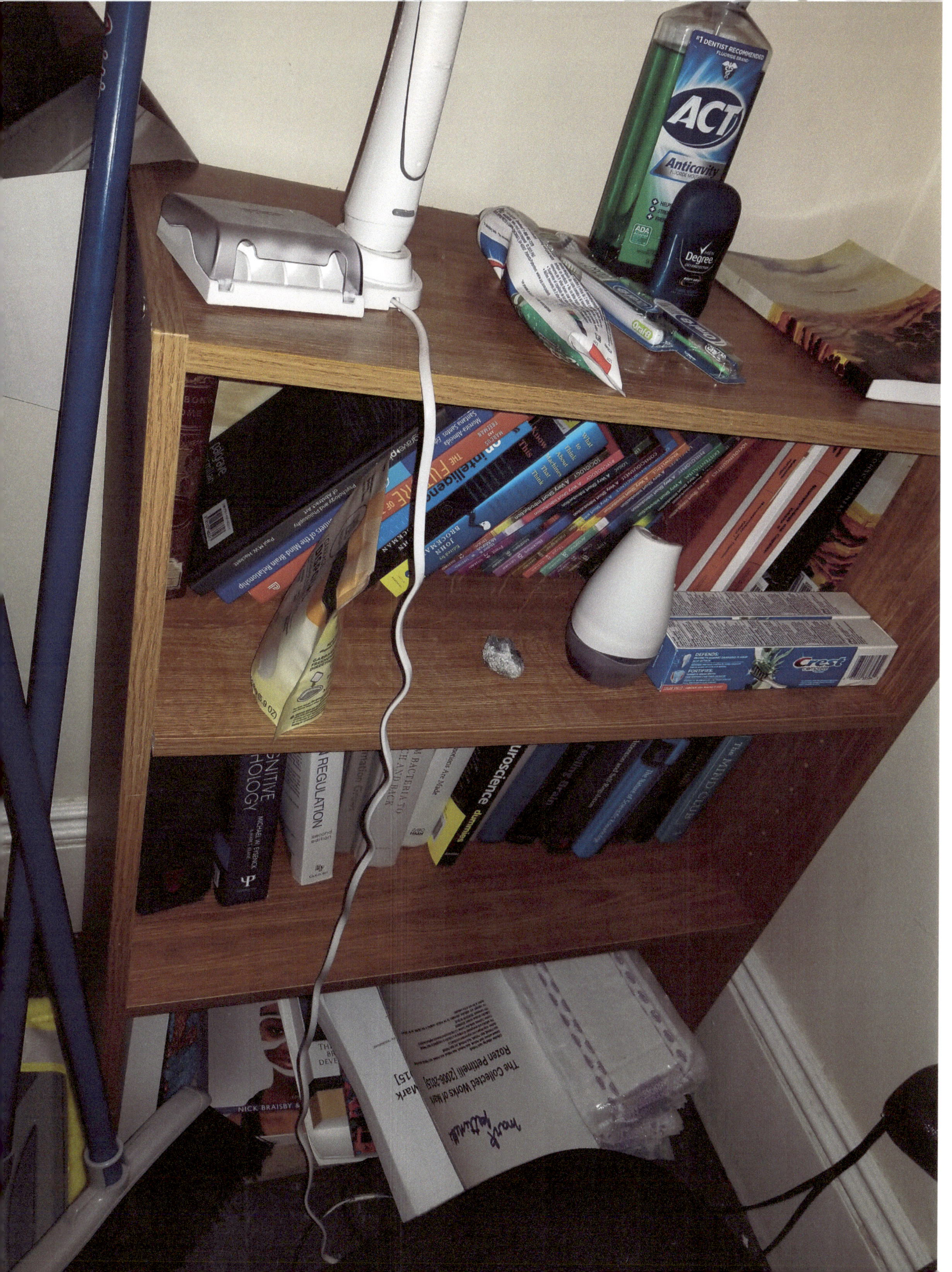

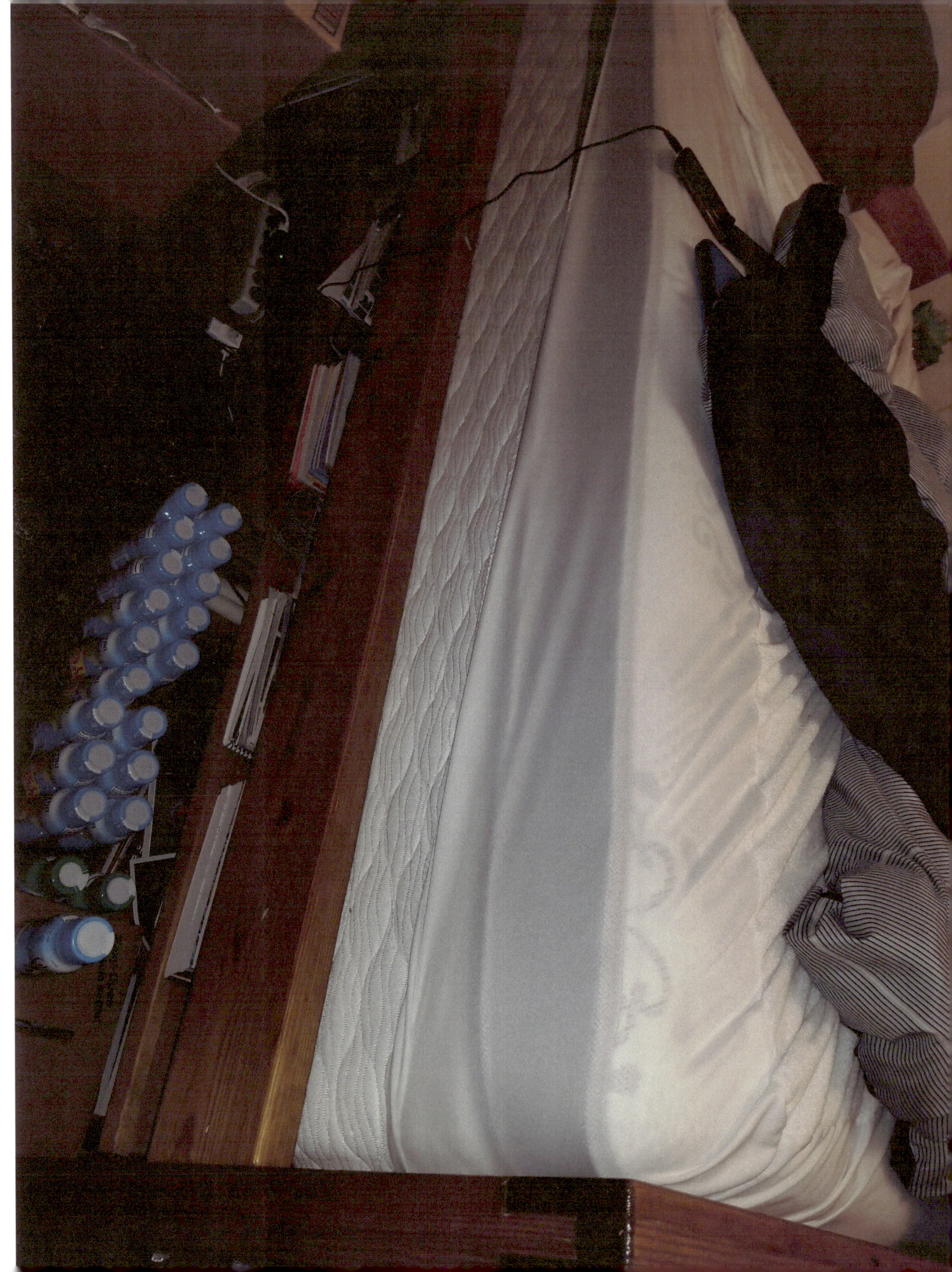

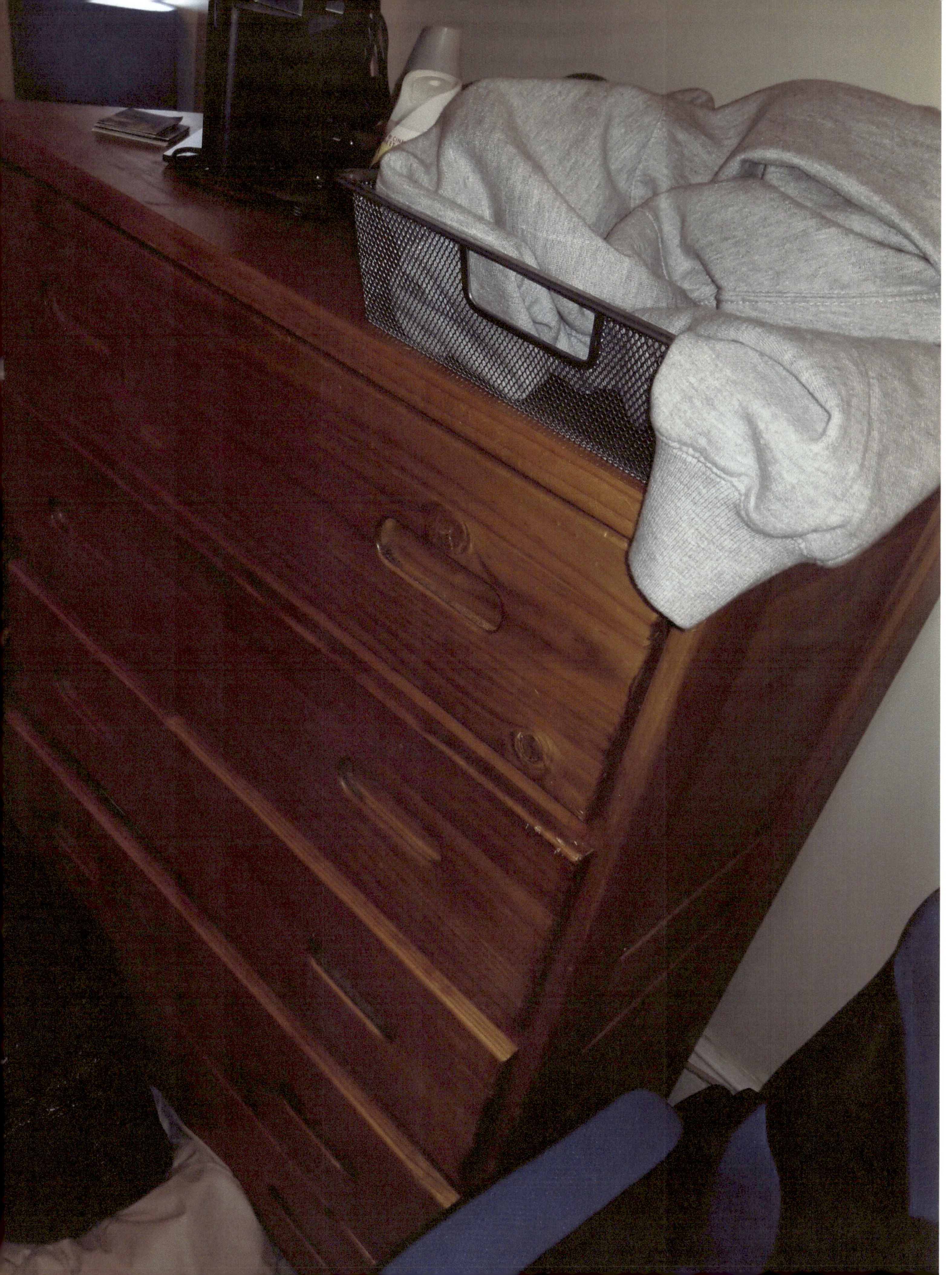

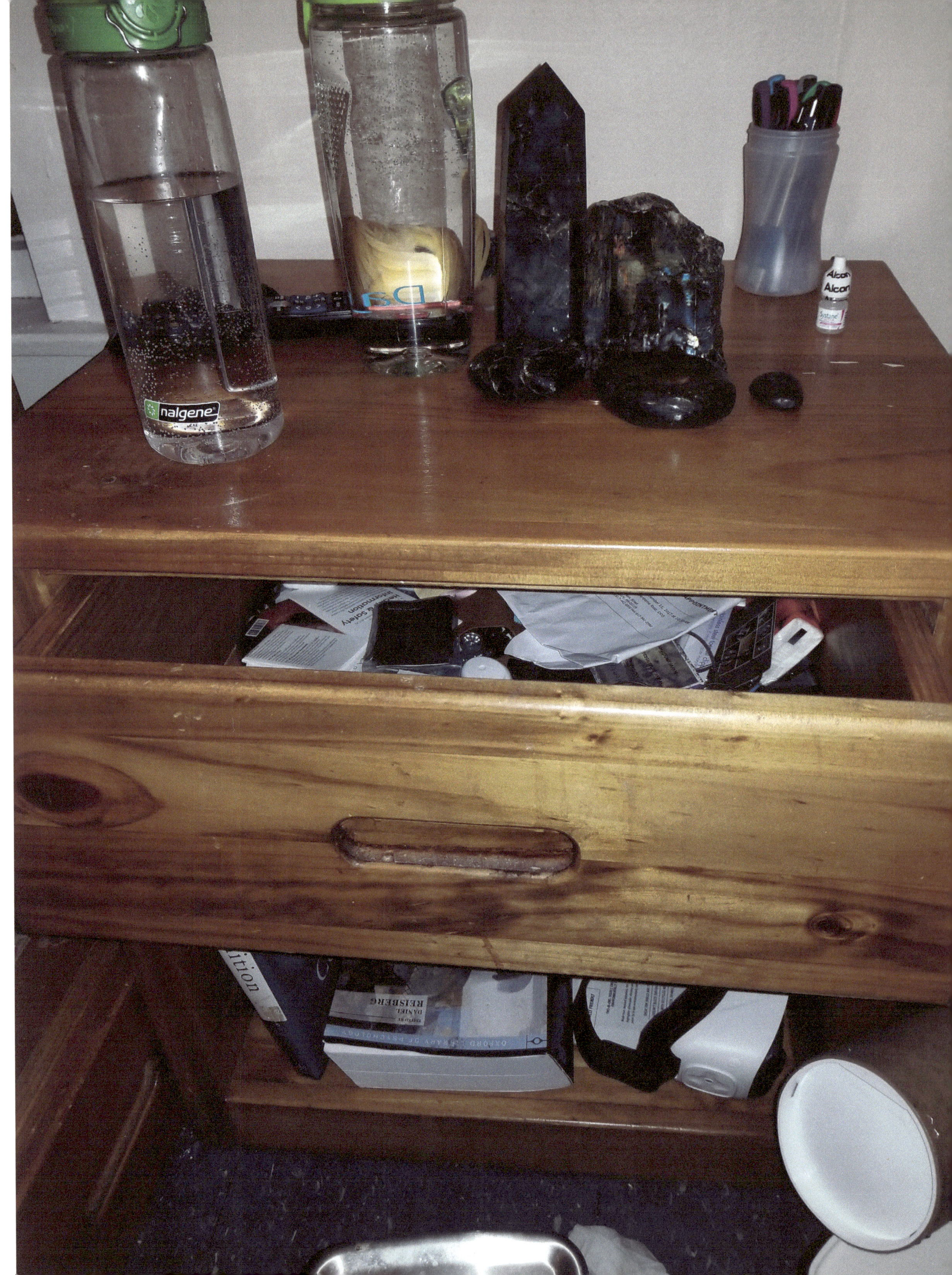

nalgene
Alcon
Systane
REISBERG
DANIEL
OXFORD
ition

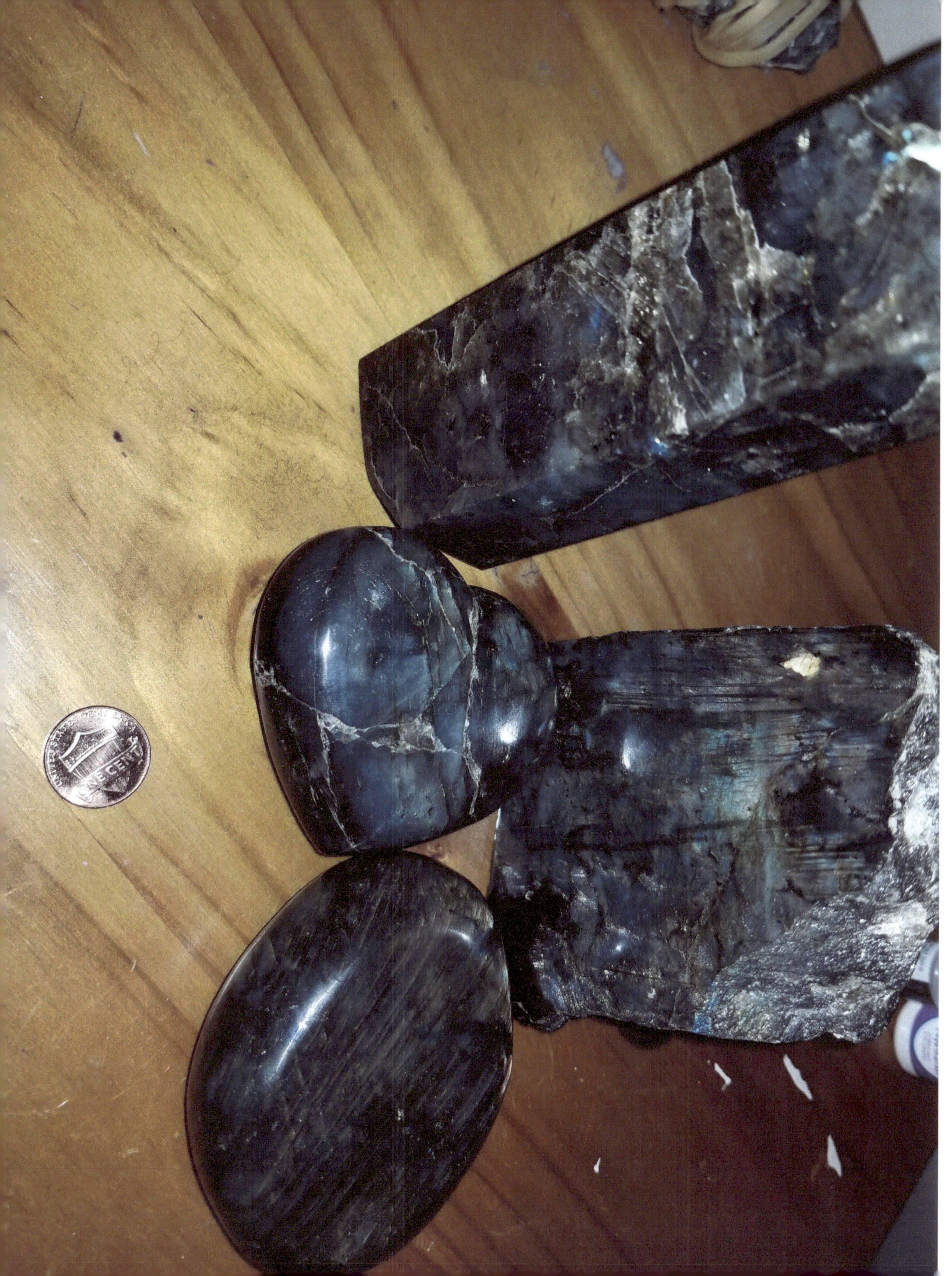

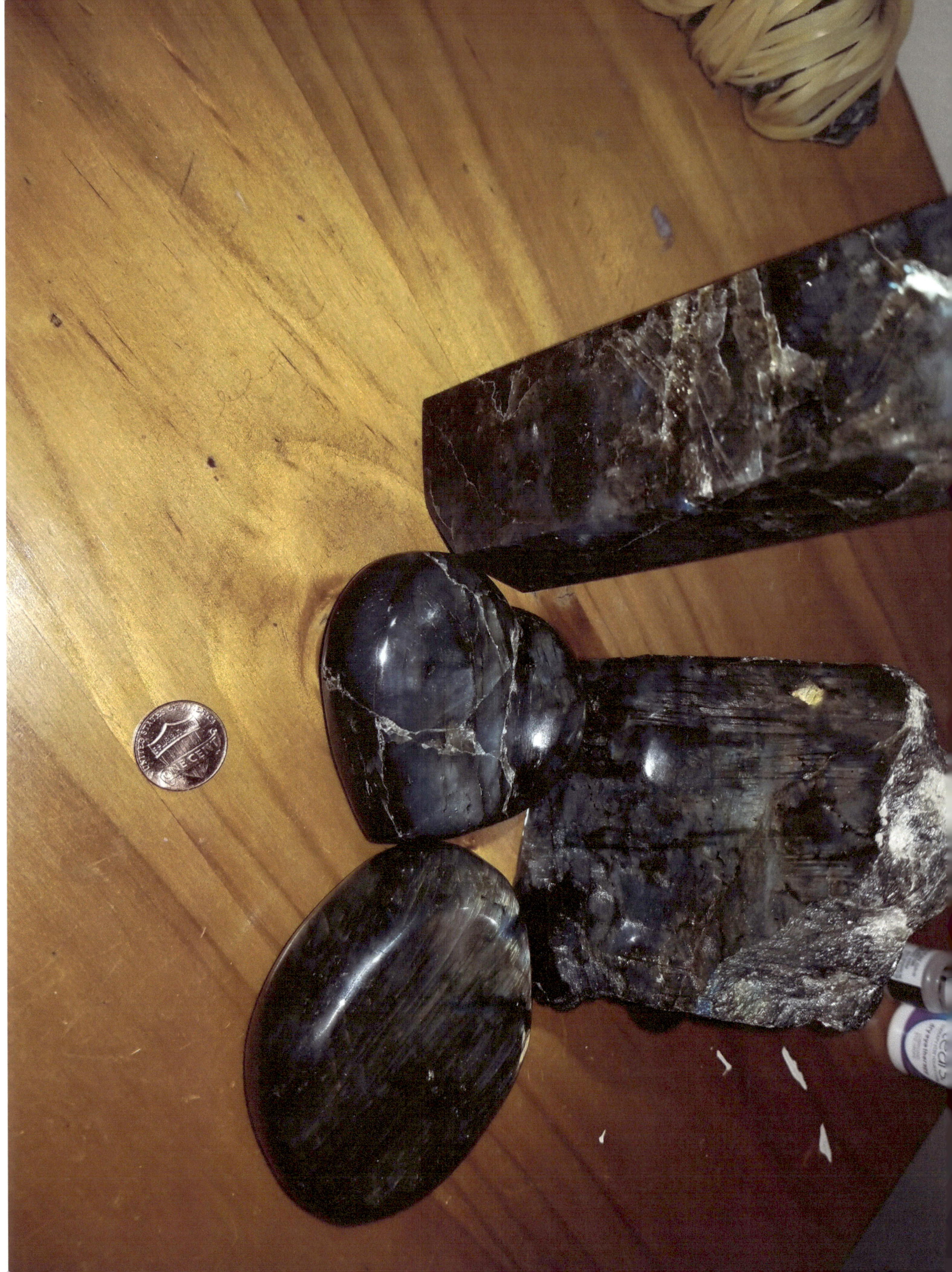

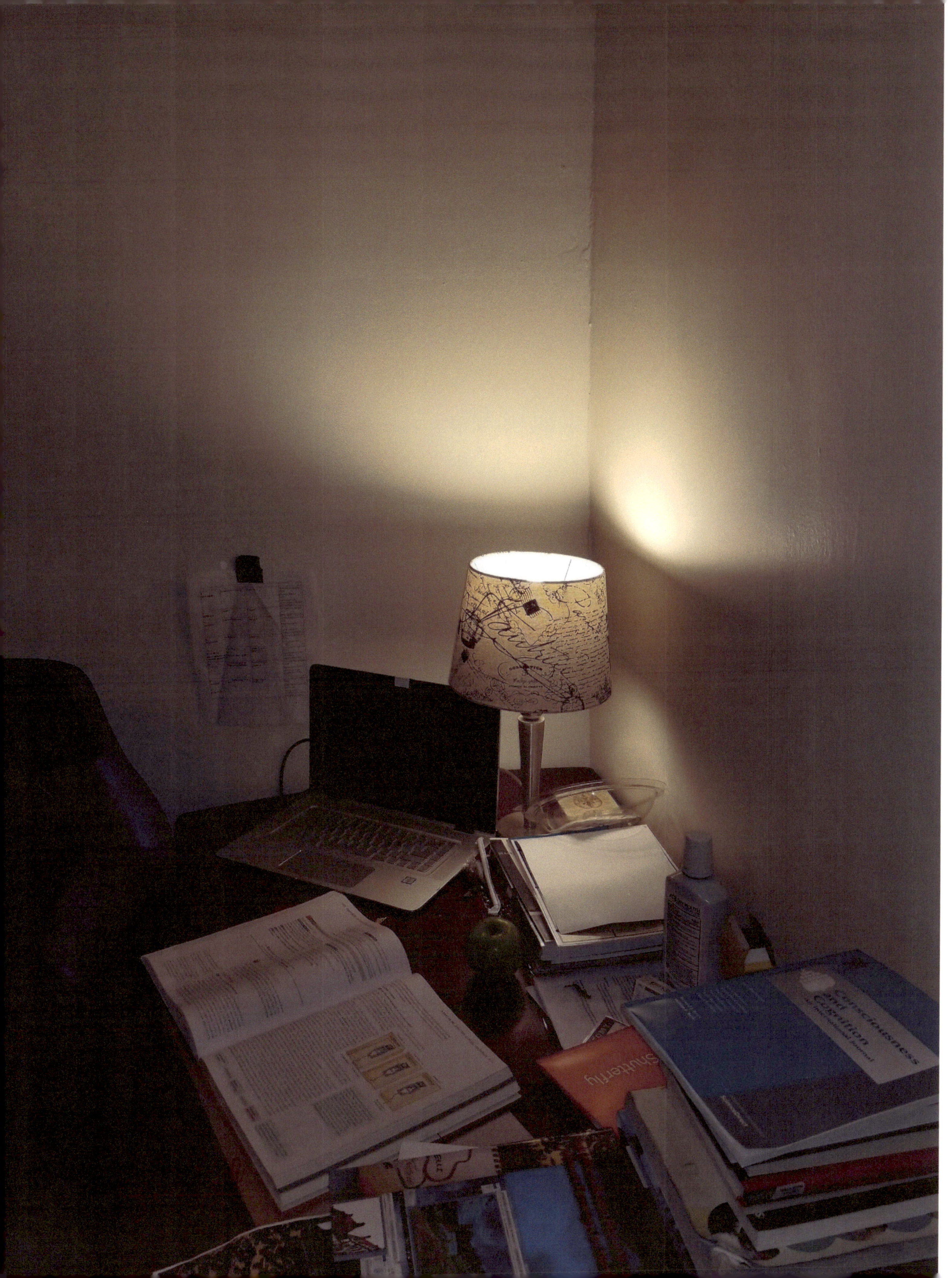

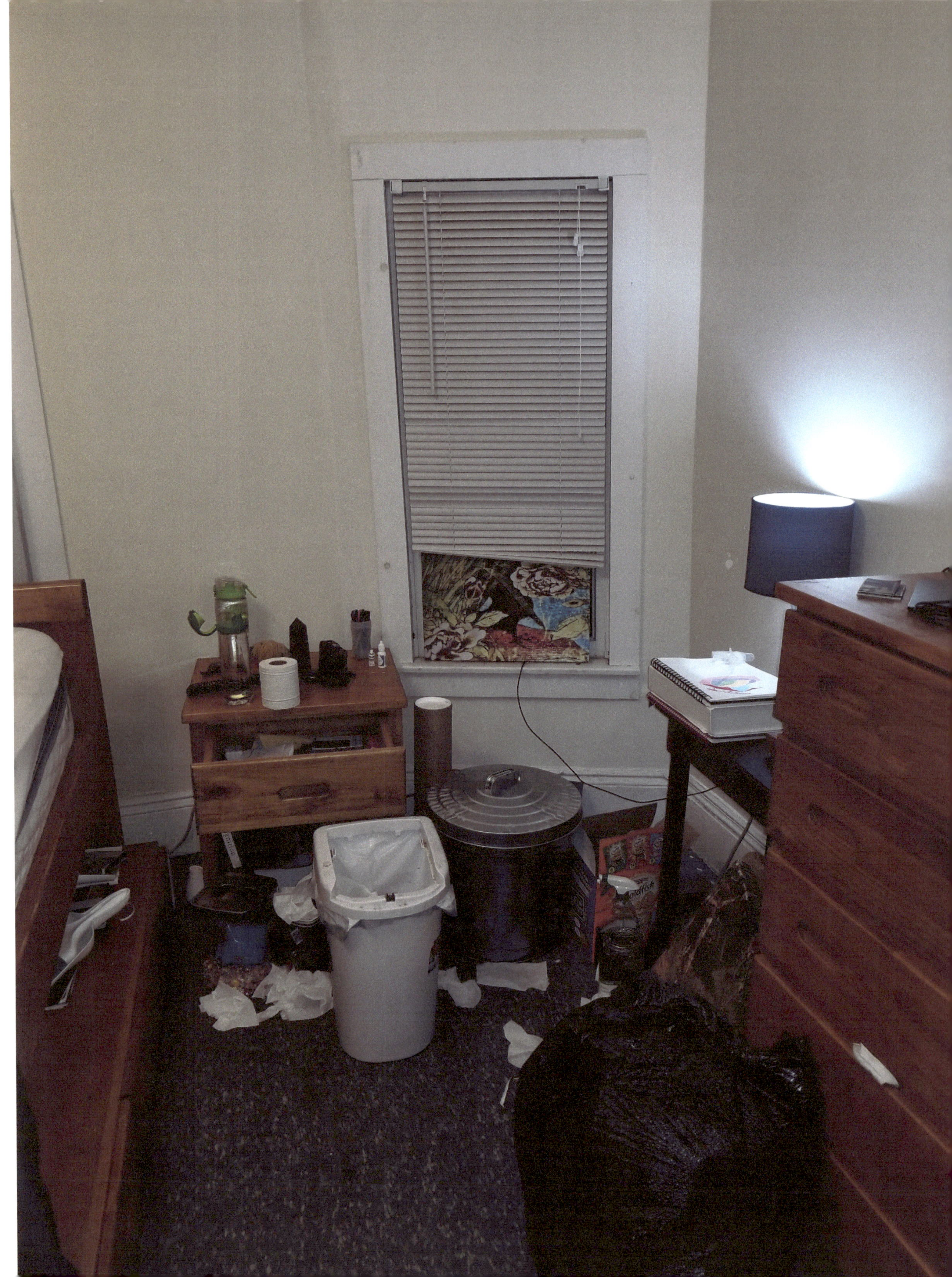

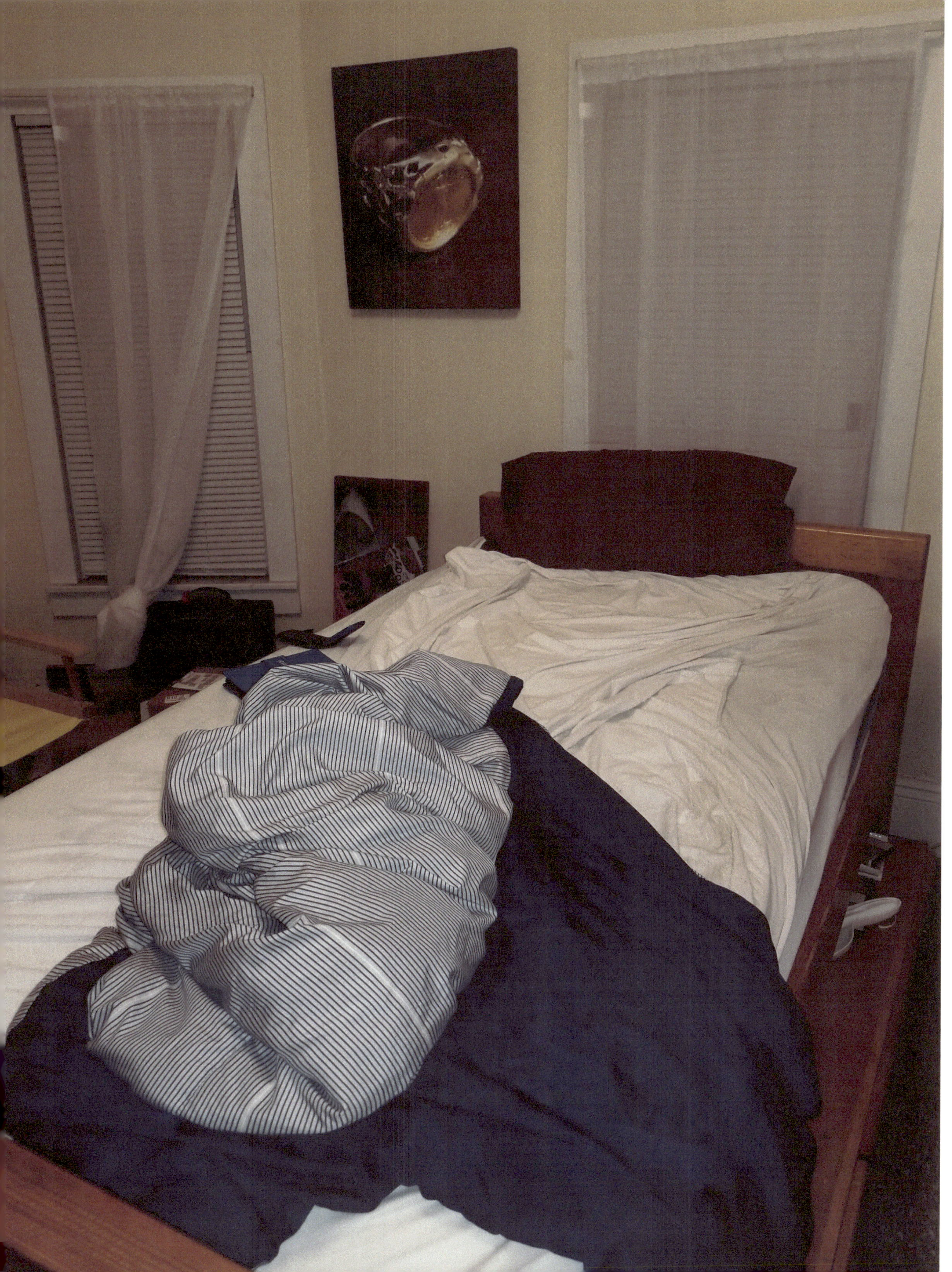

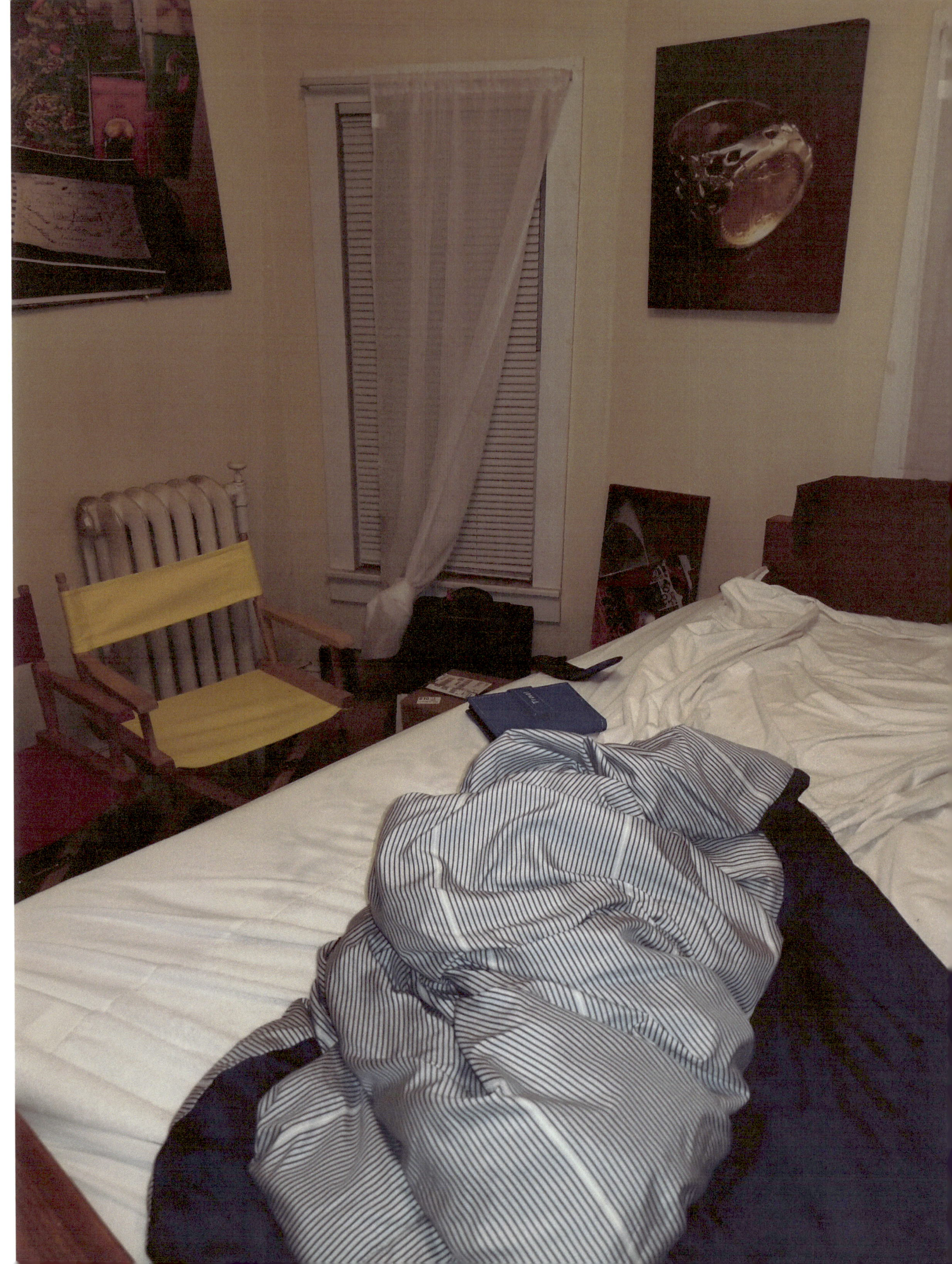

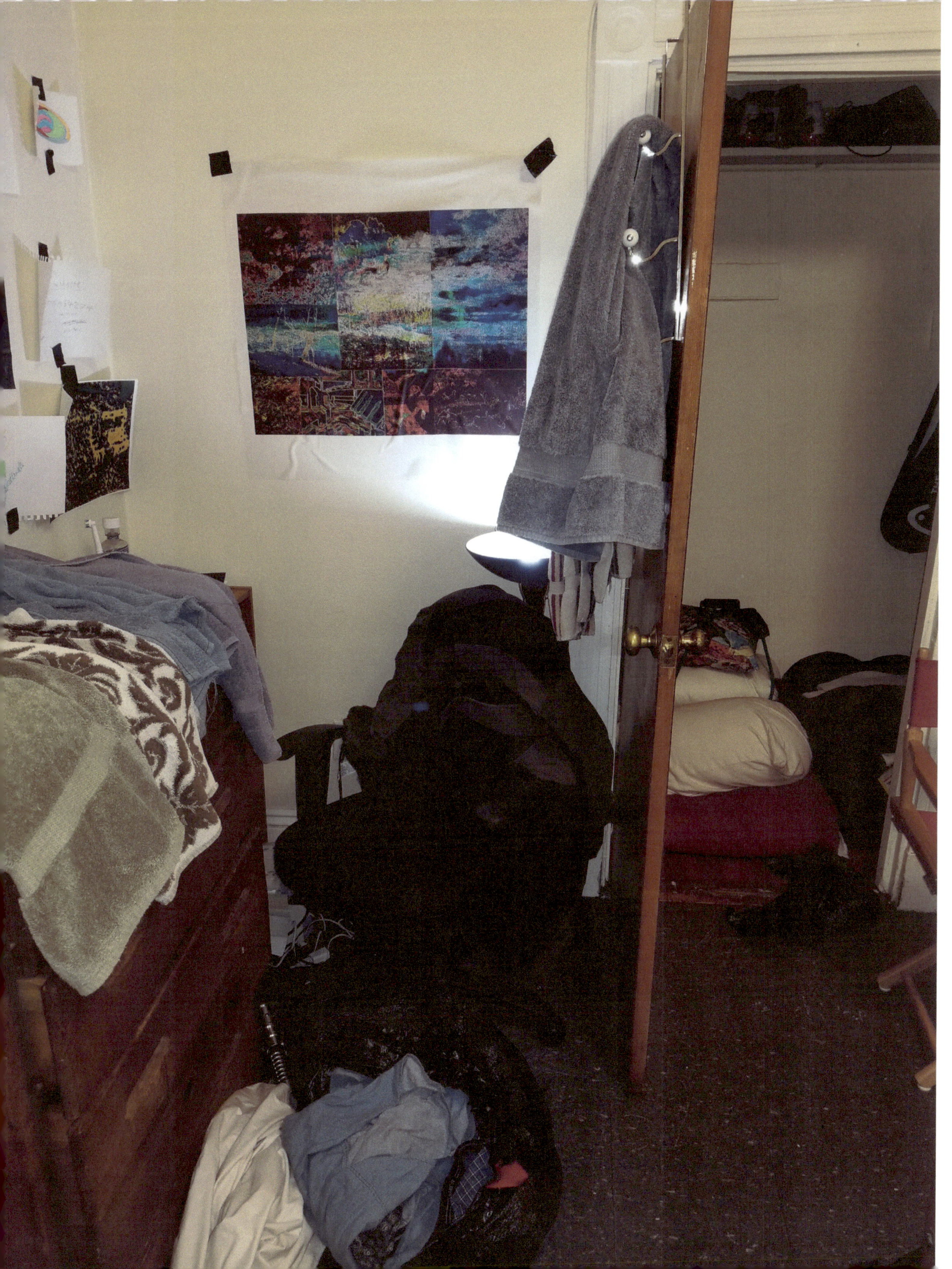

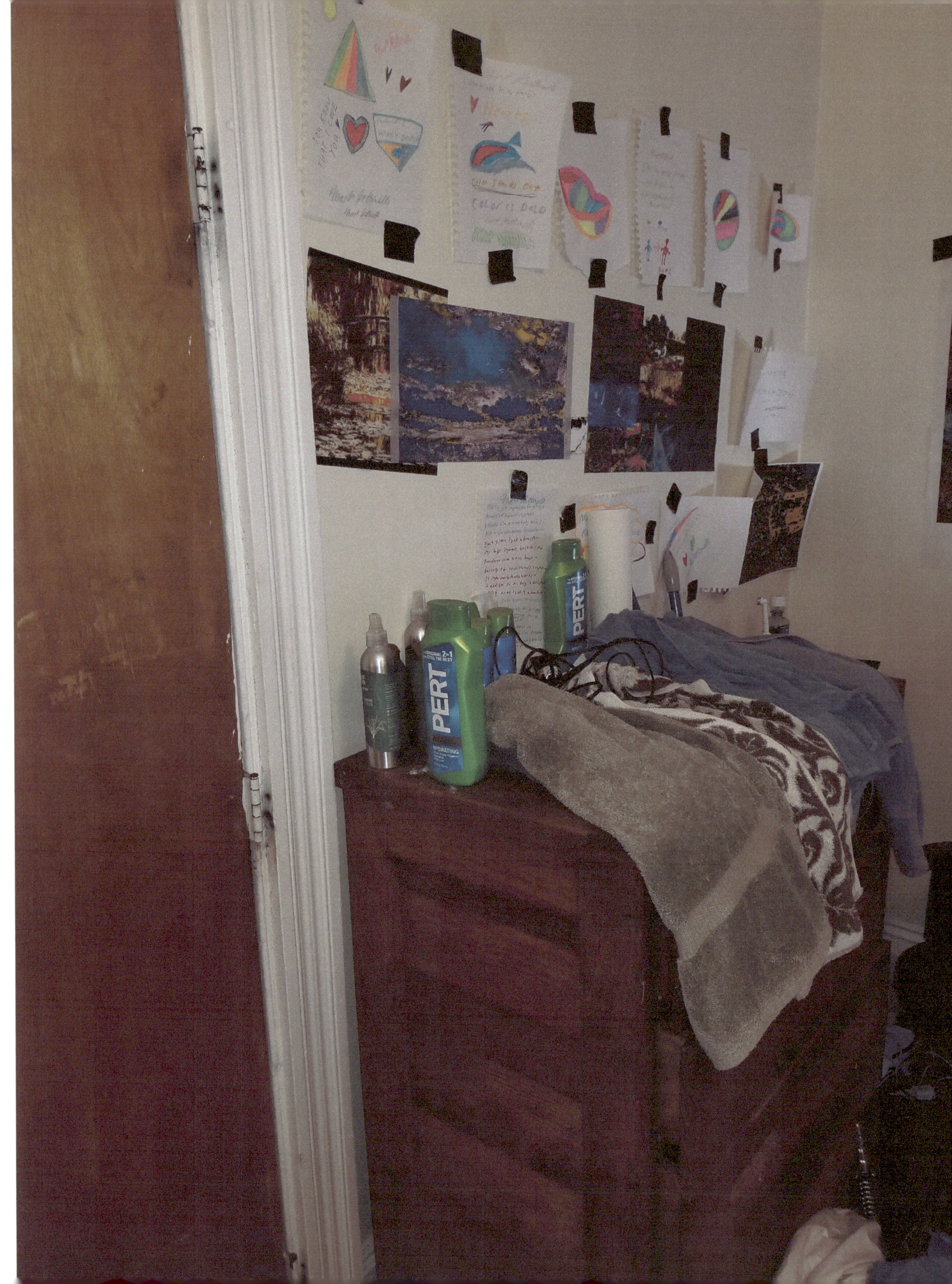

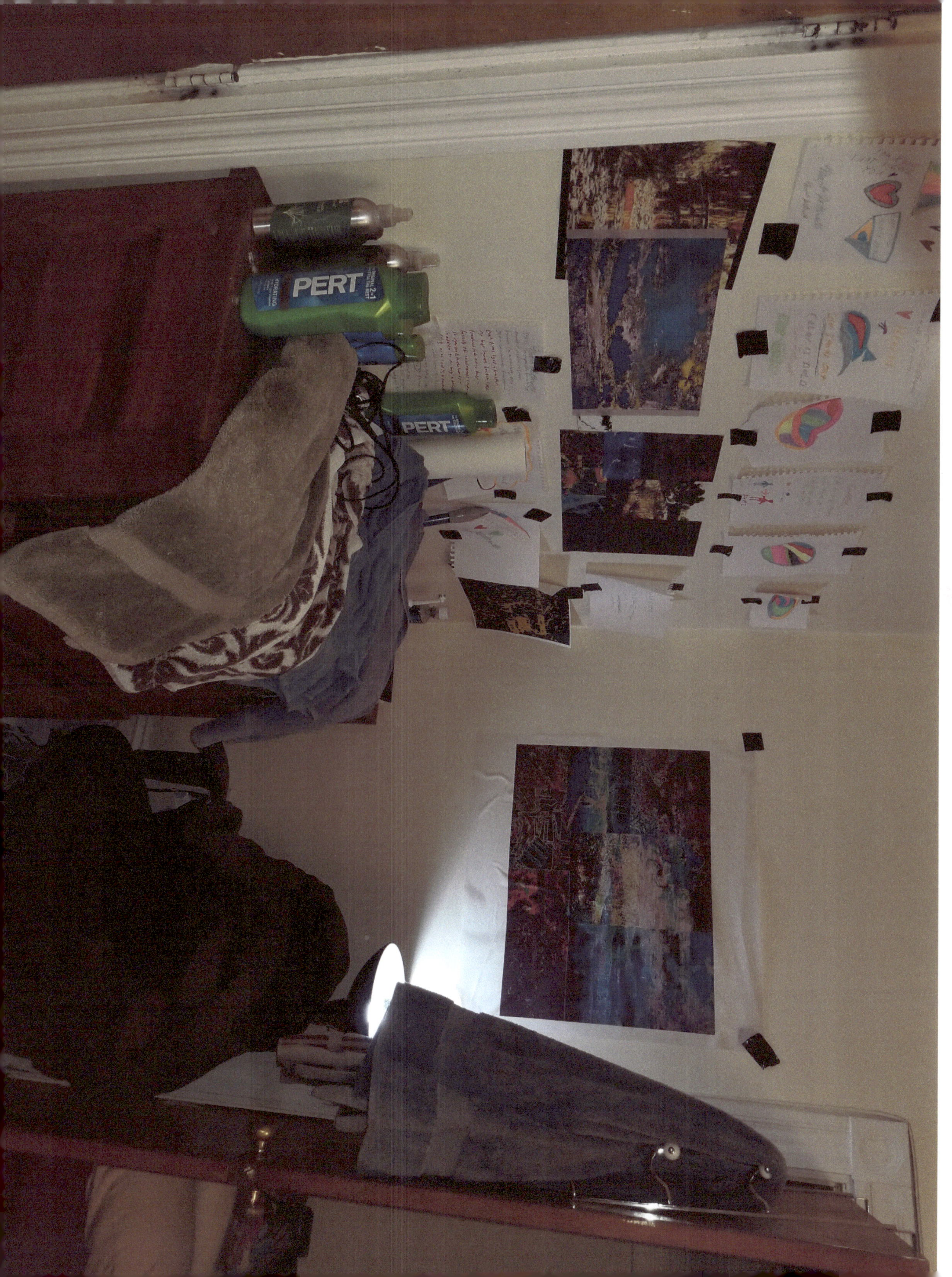

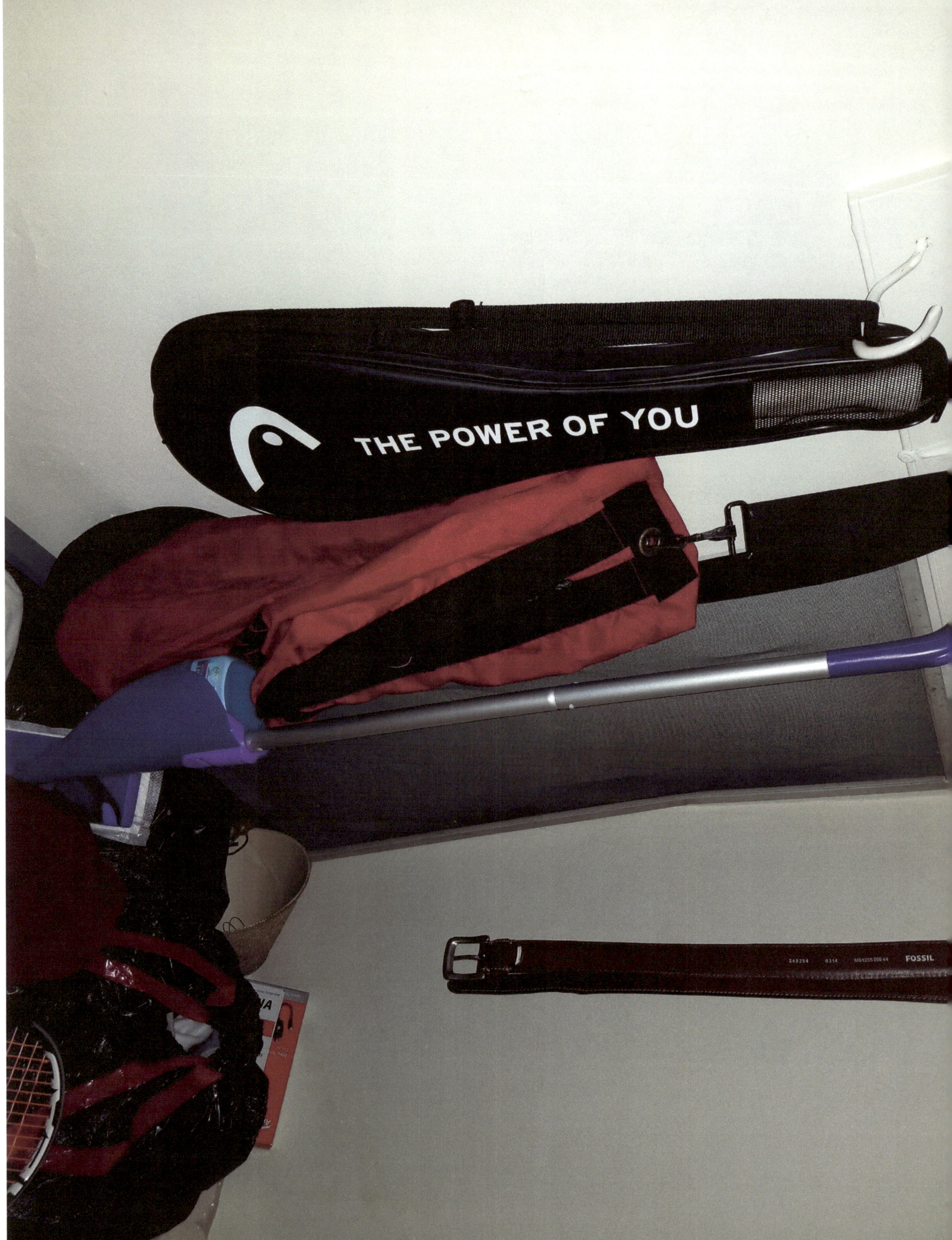
THE POWER OF YOU
248234    0314    MB1255 200 44    FOSSIL

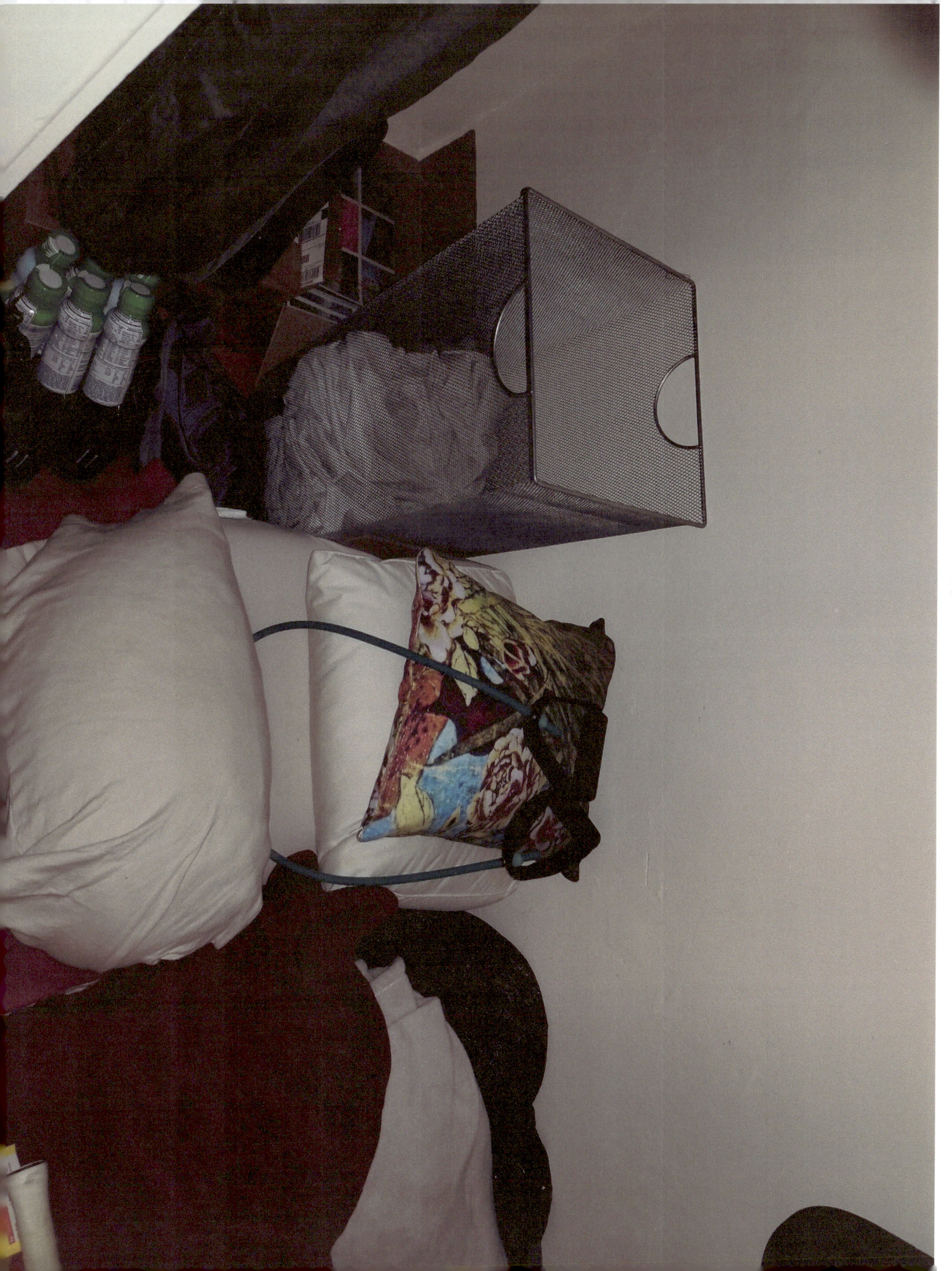

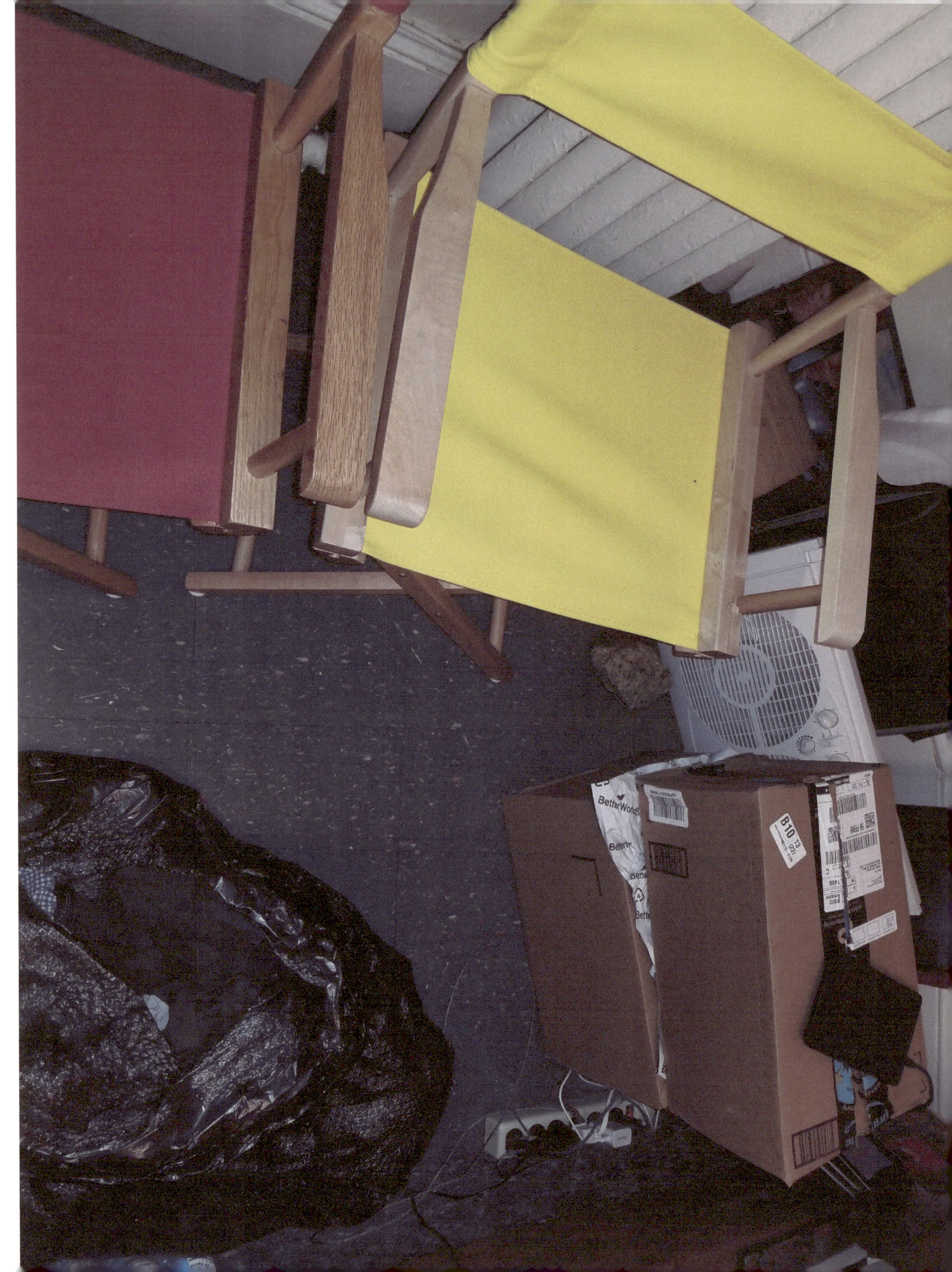

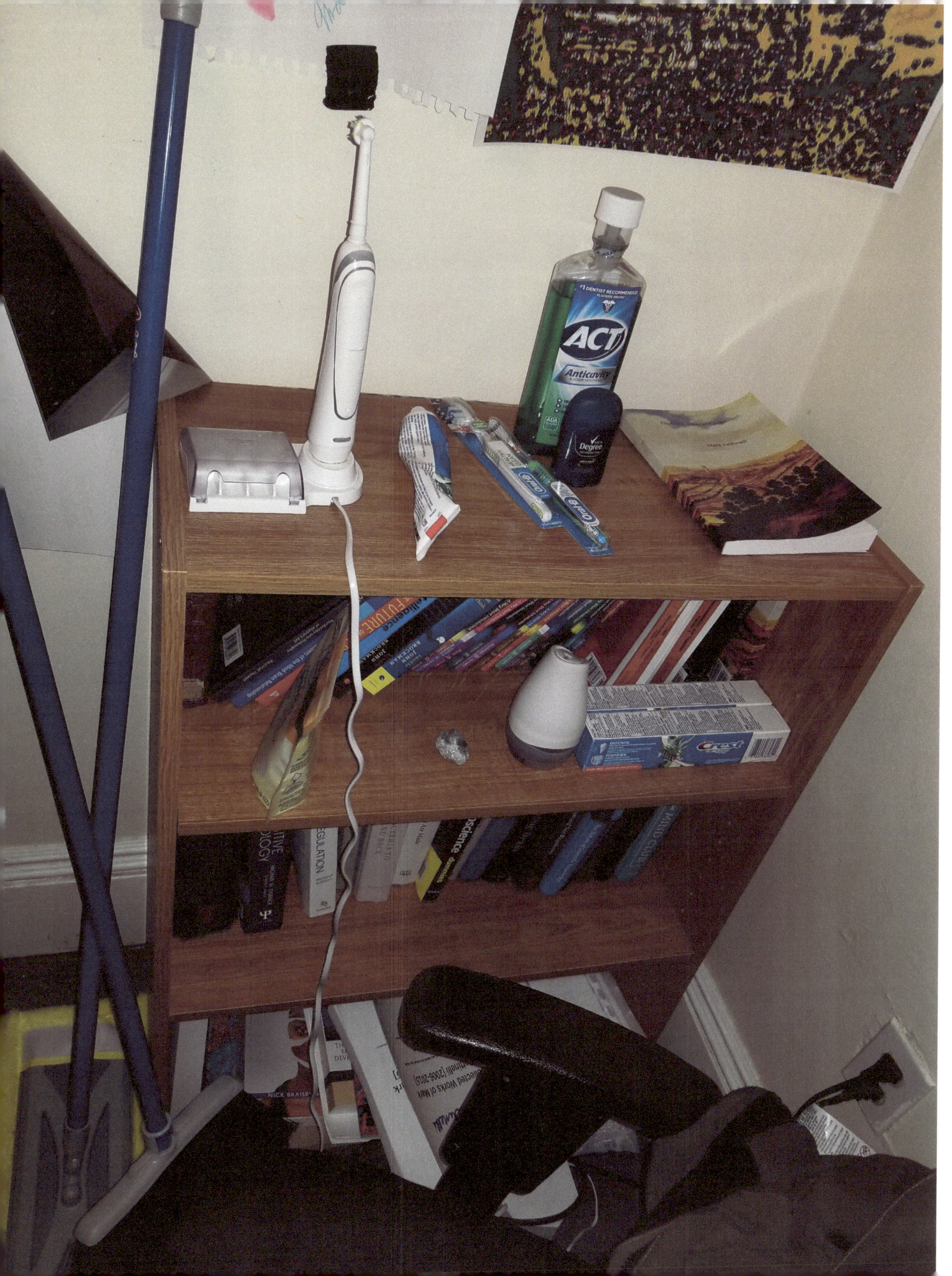

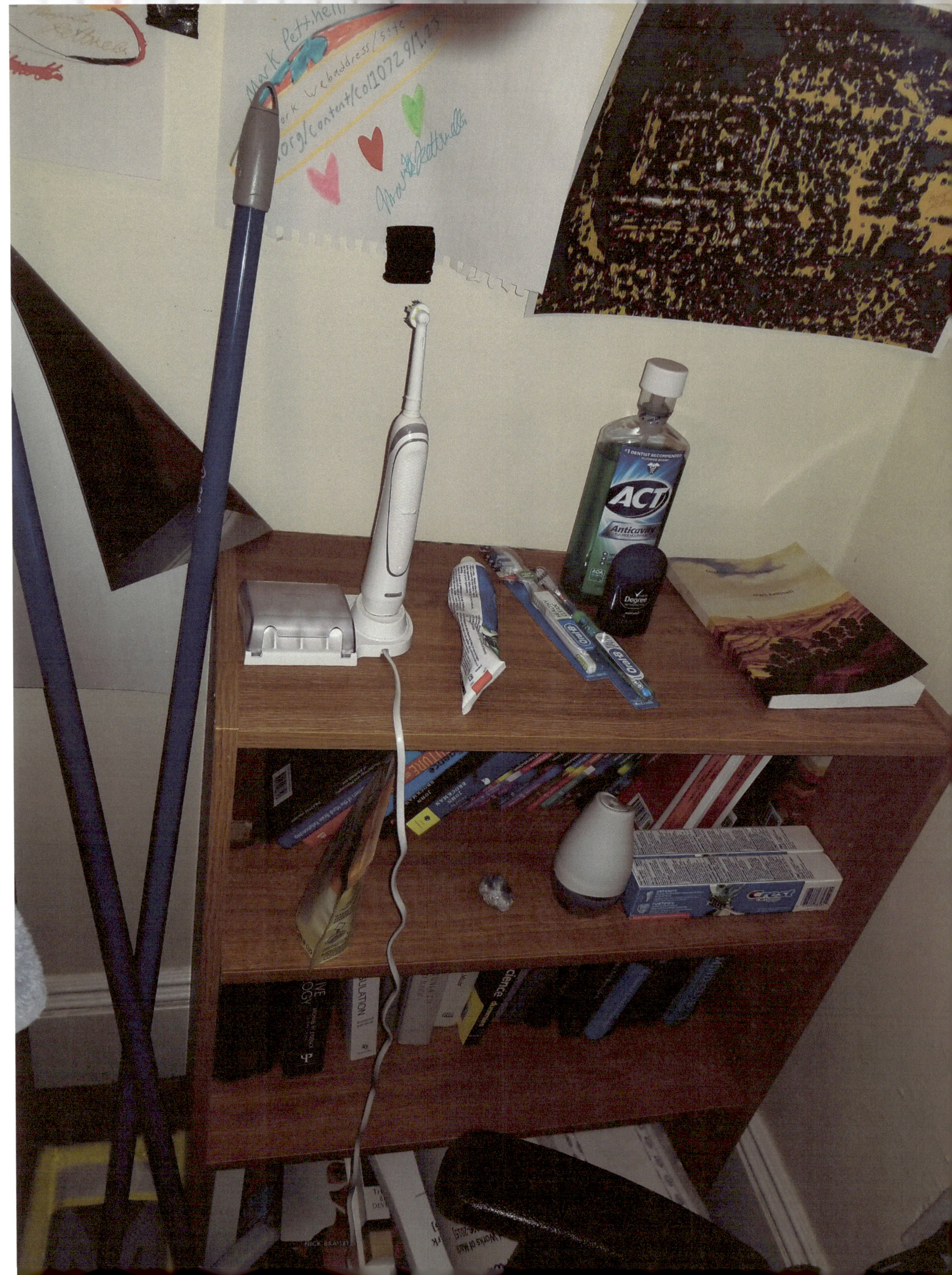

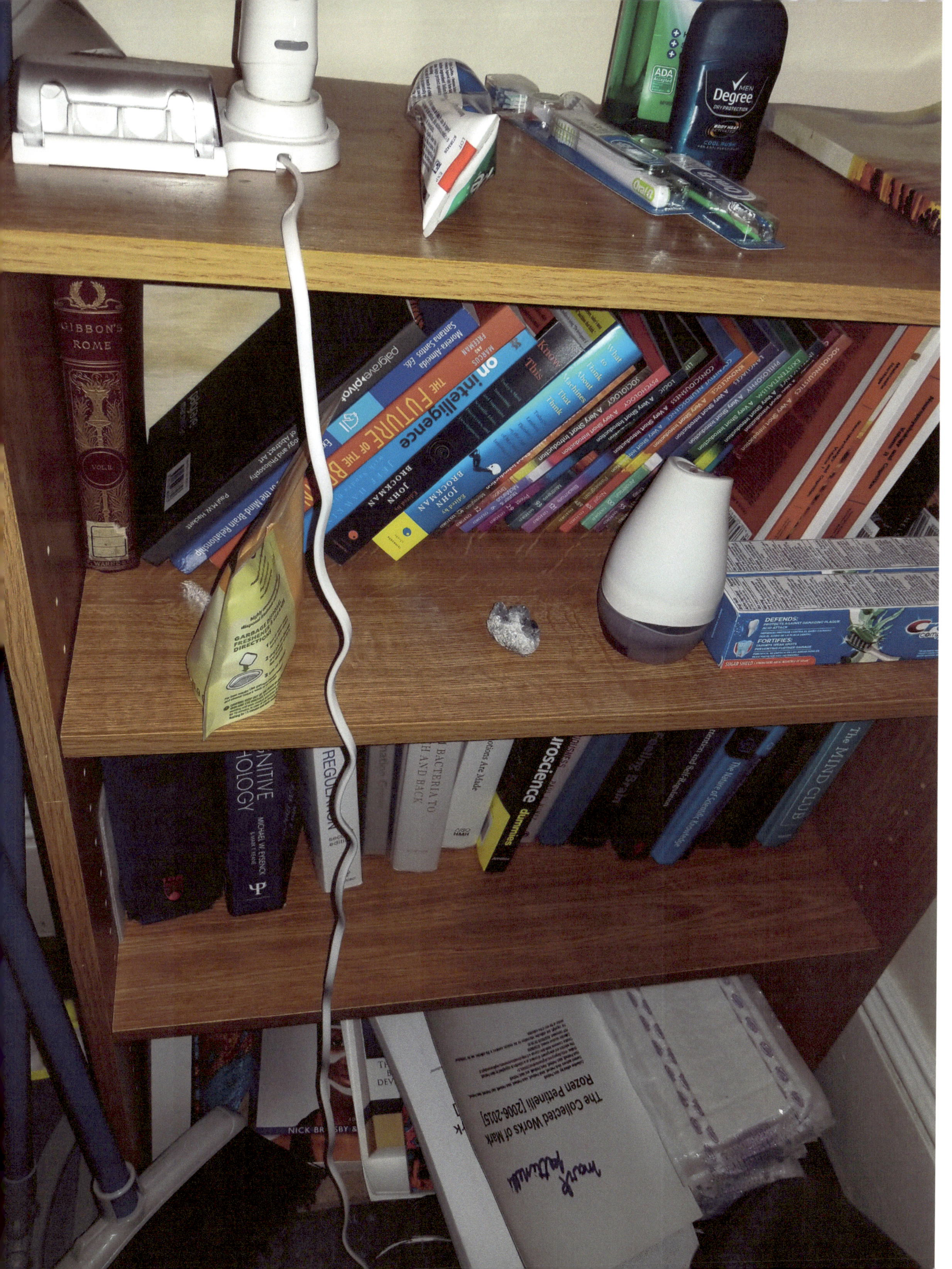

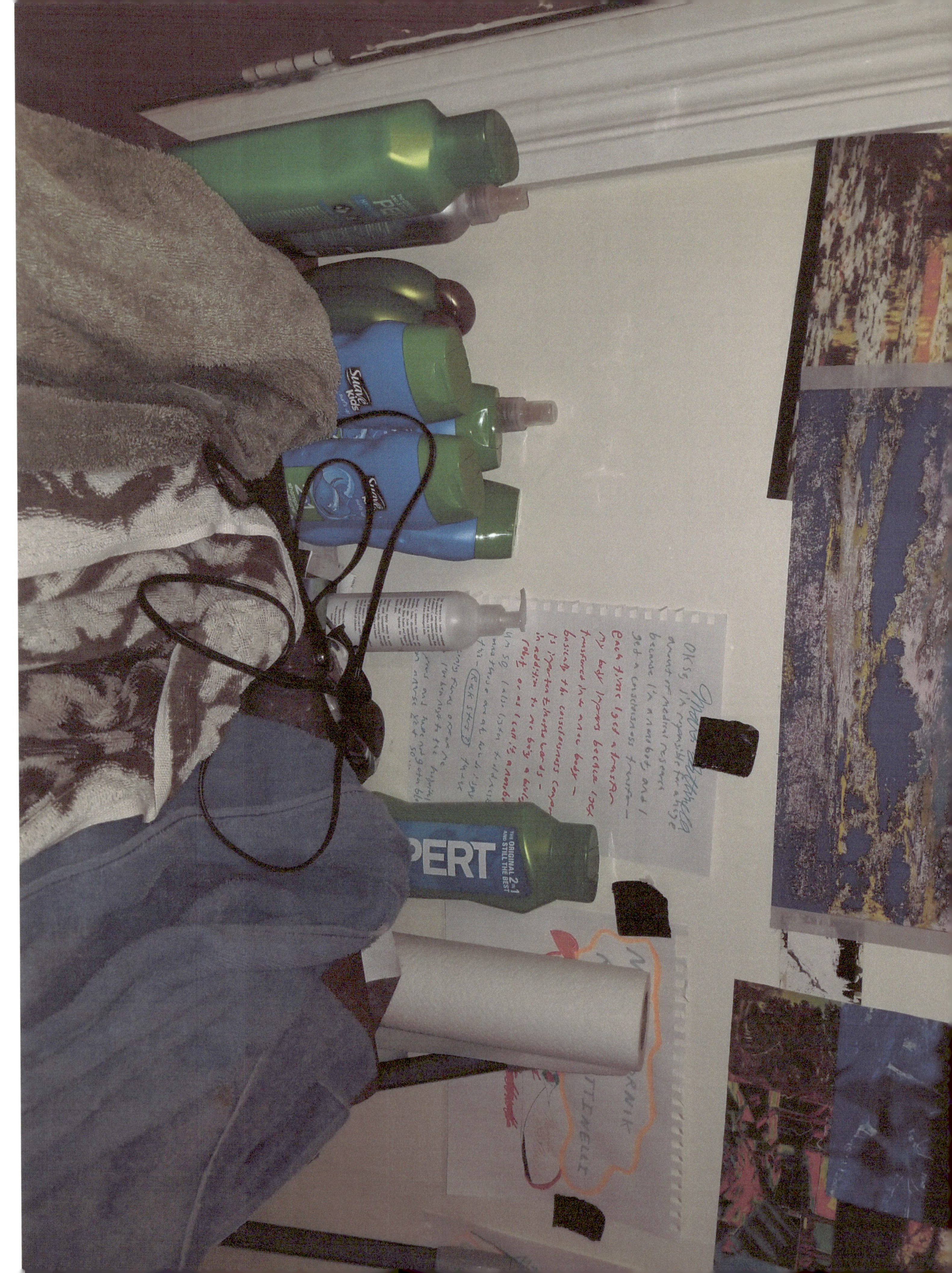

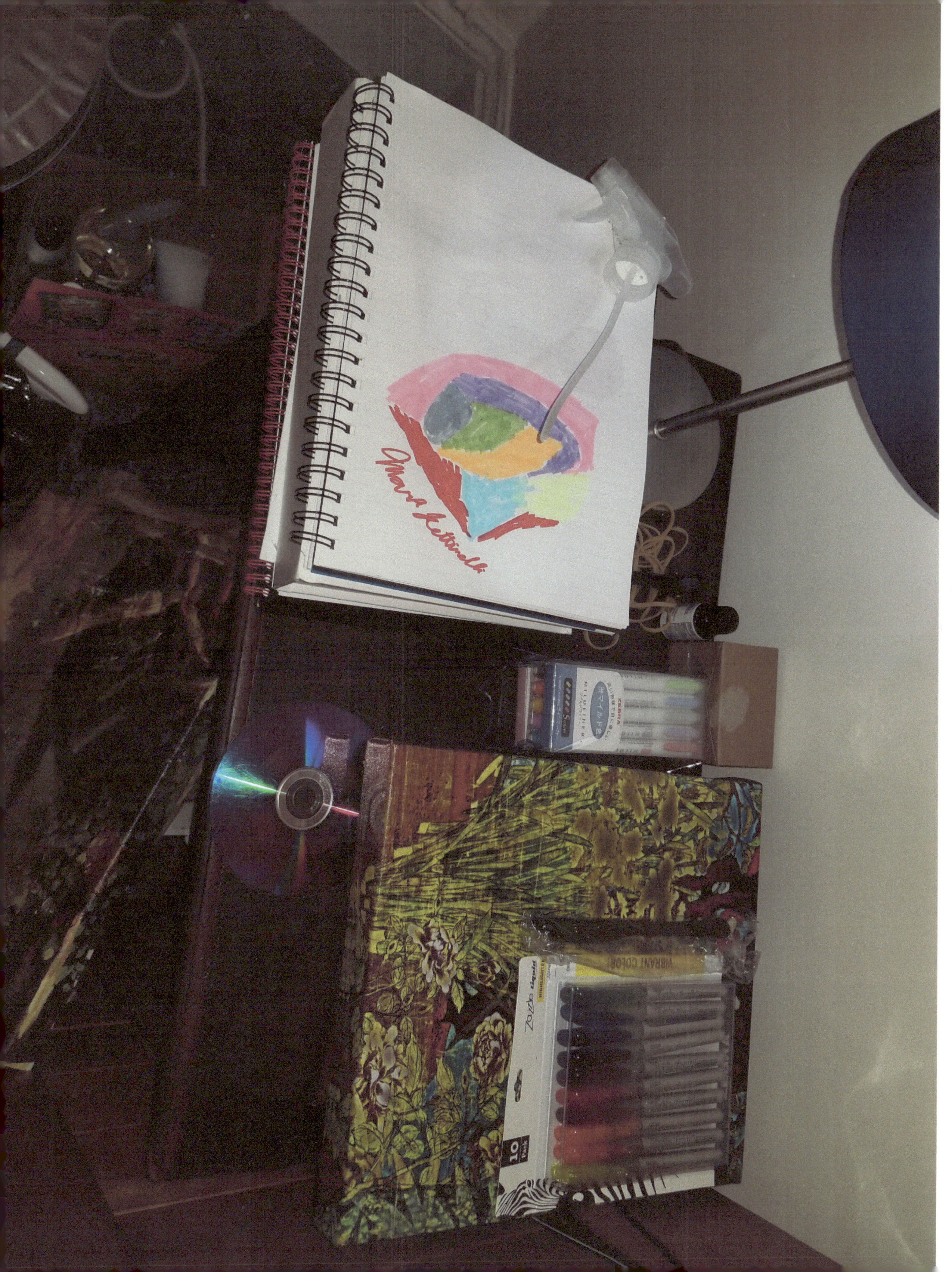

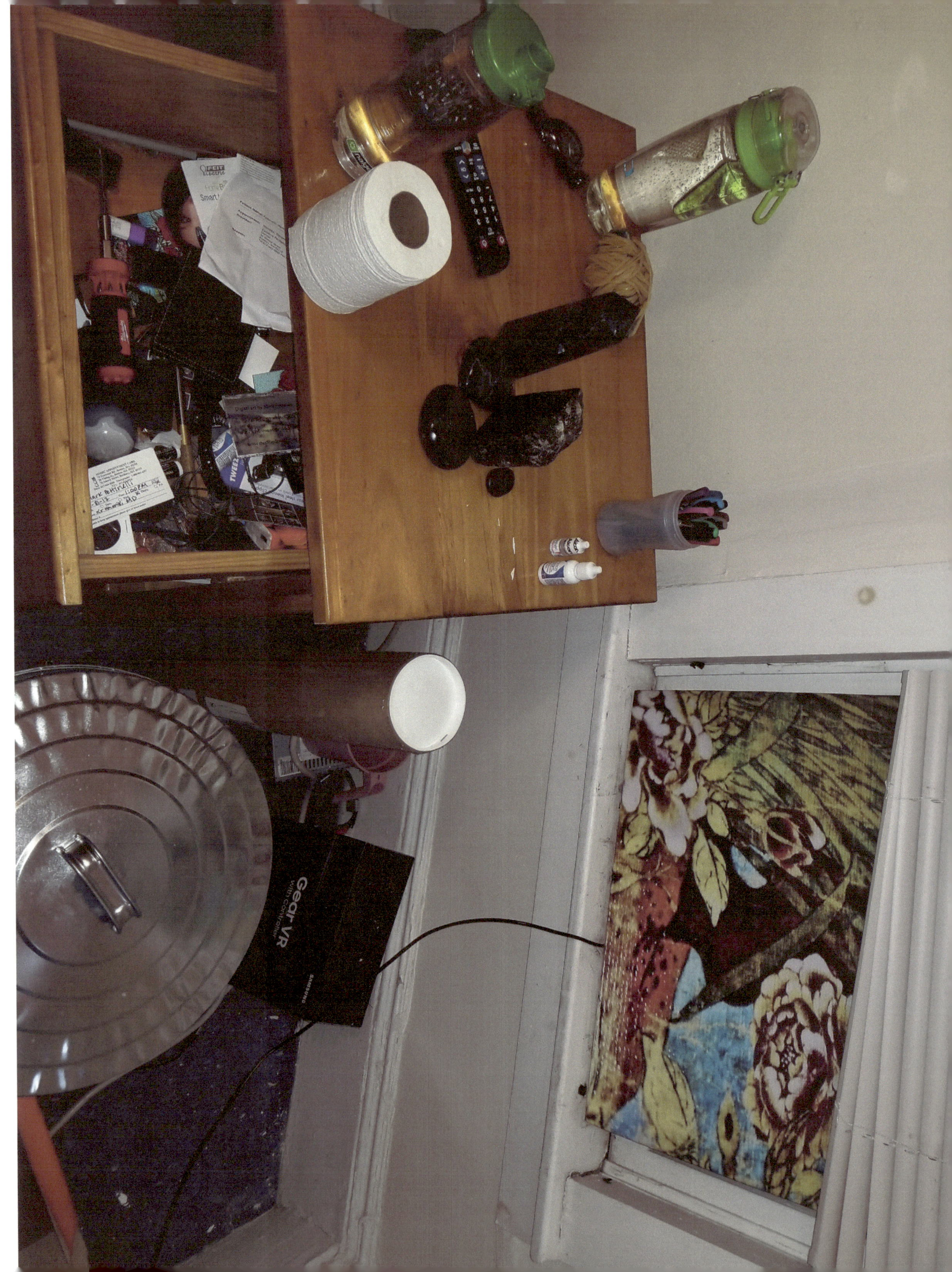